The Subtle Art of Strategy

THE SUBTLE ART OF STRATEGY

Organizational Planning in Uncertain Times

Ian Wilson

Westport, Connecticut
London

Library of Congress Cataloging-in-Publication Data

Wilson, Ian, 1925 June 16–
    The subtle art of strategy : organizational planning in uncertain times / by Ian Wilson.
    Includes bibliographical references and index.
    ISBN 1–56720–435–X (alk. paper)
      1. Strategic planning. 2. Business planning. I. Title.
HD30.28.W555   2003
658.4′012—dc21   2003048231

British Library Cataloguing in Publication Data is available.

Library of Congress Catalog Card Number: 2003048231
ISBN: 1–56720–435–X

First published in 2003

Praeger Publishers, 88 Post Road West, Westport, CT 06881
An imprint of Greenwood Publishing Group, Inc.
www.praeger.com

Printed in the United States of America

The paper used in this book complies with the
Permanent Paper Standard issued by the National
Information Standards Organization (Z39.48–1984).

10 9 8 7 6 5 4 3 2 1

I want to dedicate this book to two individuals, from quite different fields, who have influenced much of my thinking in this field:

Reginald H. ("Reg") Jones, former chairman and CEO of GE, who led the company in a pioneering venture into the then unexplored territory of strategic planning

and

The late Donald N. Michael, professor at the University of Michigan, who reminded us that, as we learn to plan, we must also plan to learn

CONTENTS

ACKNOWLEDGMENTS

As with my previous work, *The New Rules of Corporate Conduct,* this book is truly the product of more than 40 years of experience in the corporate and consulting worlds. As such, it owes a great deal to the stimulation and challenges I have received from those with whom I have worked over this long, exciting, and often tempestuous period.

At General Electric, I had my initiation into the mysteries of strategic planning in the early 1970s, when that company, under the leadership of Reg Jones, made its pioneering venture into that then new field. It was there that I first learned just how complex strategy really is—far more complex than the simplistic, largely quantitative tools of that time would admit. I gained more than I realized at the time from working on a daily basis with such insightful minds as Charlie Reed, Stan Gault, Jack McKitterick, Bill Rothschild, Bill Reed, and Kurt Hellfach. Although I moved to SRI International in 1980, and so did not have the opportunity of working with Jack Welch when he took over as CEO, my thinking on this subject was sharpened by our periodic exchange of letters over the course of the next 20 years, until his retirement in 2001.

My stay at SRI brought me into close touch with many stimulating individuals, both at the Institute and in the many corporations around the world with whom we had consulting relationships. This was, for me, truly a global experience, covering the United Kingdom, Norway, France, Finland, Japan, Singapore, Taiwan, Venezuela, and Argentina, as well, of course, as Canada and the United States. It was an experience that gave me a broader viewpoint that I might otherwise have developed. In particular, I want to acknowledge the personal and professional friendships that I enjoyed with Pat Henry, Ken Colmen, Tom Boyce, Tom Mandel, and Eilif Trondsen at SRI, and the many individuals in client corporations who shared their experience and insight with me through their participation in my survey of thinking and practices in the strategic management field.

Like many others in this field, I have benefited immeasurably from the thinking and writing of pioneers such as Ken Andrews, Igor Ansoff, Henry Mintzberg, Michael Porter, Gary Hamel, and others listed in the bibliography. On a more personal basis, I have enjoyed provocative conversations over the years with Bernard Taylor at Henley Management College; Warren Bennis, Burt Nanus, and Jim O'Toole at the University of Southern California; George Steiner, when he was at UCLA; Liam Fahey and Robert Randall, whose *The Portable MBA in Strategy* has become a bible for many practitioners; Bill Halal at George Washington University; Pentti Malaska and Markku Wilenius at Turku University, Finland; and my dear friend, the late Pierre Wack of Royal Dutch/Shell.

Some of the materials in the following chapters has appeared in an earlier format in such publications as *Long Range Planning, Planning Review,* and *Strategy & Leadership.* I am most grateful to the editors of these publications, as well as to Eric Valentine, my publisher at Quorum Books, for giving me a platform on which to articulate and, over the years, refine my views on this important subject.

Finally, as always, I owe more than I can adequately express—probably more even than I realize—to my wife, Adrianne. Throughout the long travail of my writing this book, she has always been at my side, inspiring and questioning, challenging and comforting. To say that I could not have written this book without her is an understatement.

Chapter 1

INTRODUCTION AND
PERSPECTIVE

Already I can imagine some of the cries of outrage that will greet the publication of this volume: "Oh, no! Not *another* book on strategic planning!" Indeed the literature on the subject is already vast, diverse, and confusing. Since the 1970s, in books, articles, conferences, and seminars, we have been treated to a bewildering array of theories and methodologies, each of which has been advanced by its author as the royal road to strategy. In their own book on the subject, *Strategy Safari: A Guided Tour through the Wilds of Strategic Management,* Henry Mintzberg and his coauthors identified 10 different schools of thought. They assert that strategy is our elephant and we are all like blind men, believing that the part we have seized on is the whole.

But strategy requires that we look at the whole, for we are dealing with the *totality* of the organization in the context of its *total* environment. Strategy is, or should be, concerned with integrating every function and every facet of an organization into a coherent whole, driven by a central dynamic, and shaped by its response to the whole array of forces—economic, competitive, social, political, and technological—that form the arena in which it operates. It is in this sense that we can safely assert that strategy is, or should be, holistic.

As I point out in chapter 4, strategy is concerned with harnessing an array of opposites and seeming contradictions—the long term and the short term; vision and execution; external relationships and internal operations; and economic constraints and social purpose. As such, it cannot be fully defined by any one of Mintzberg's schools of thought. It is far too complex, far too subtle, to be constrained by such a narrow definition. It is an art—a subtle and demanding art—far more than a science.

My aim in writing this book has been to explore this complexity—to define and explain it, not to simplify it—and to suggest how we might best deal with it. This is not a "how-to" book in the traditional sense, a by-the-numbers cookbook for strategic planning, for most of the factors that make for success in strategy do not lend themselves to a how-to formula. Rather, if I were to try to categorize this book, I might say it is a "what-to" and "why-to" book. By this I mean that it attempts to define exactly *what* strategy, with all its intricacies, entails, and *why* now, more than ever, we need to think and act strategically.

This last point, indeed, is my response to the many of those who would argue that strategic planning is now impractical and irrelevant in the post–September 11, 2001, world. They note, correctly, that the world of the 1990s has been turned upside down and that the level of uncertainty confronting us has increased by an order of magnitude. Indeed, it is uncertainty, rather than change, per se, that has become the dominant characteristic of our age. And, in an increasingly interconnected world, there is no escape from this fact, no place left to hide. But the naysayers are *not* correct in then asserting that our inability to forecast the future and deal with uncertainty makes planning impossible and strategy a luxury we cannot afford.

On the contrary, I would argue, our need for thinking and acting strategically has never been greater. In a relatively stable world, planning is easy, but less necessary, for continuing to do more or less what we are doing today might be all the strategy we need. It is precisely when we cannot predict what we will encounter—and when sheer survival, not merely success, is at issue—that we most need a clear sense of vision of where we want to go and how we can get there. And *that*, in simplest terms, is the essence of strategy.

The bottom line is this: In conditions such as we are facing now, a dynamic, realistic and responsive strategy is the sine qua non for success. Without such a strategy, any organization will be like a ship adrift, without a rudder, on a stormy sea. And to develop this strategy, we need some form of planning system, not (as so often in the past) as a straitjacket, but rather as a means of channeling and focusing management's thinking on the key issues confronting the organization.

No doubt it will be a different kind of strategic planning from that which many organizations currently employ. Most certainly, our planning will have to learn to deal with uncertainty more explicitly and more constructively than it does now (see chapter 6, "Strategy in Uncertain Times"). Most managers are spooked by uncertainty, seeing it only as a threat to both their organization's future and their own competence ("If you don't *know*, you are *in*competent!"). To find the opportunities that lie hidden in this uncertainty requires a radical change of attitude and the skillful use of scenarios and other similar methodologies.

Then, too, both strategy and the planning process will have to become much more flexible than they are now. Planning will become a continuous activity (plan, execute, feedback, replan) as organizations learn their way into the future rather than remain tied to the artificial constraints of an annual planning calendar. And the execution of strategy will require vastly greater flexibility and initiative on the part of managers—not only at the higher levels of management, but throughout the organization—in order to deal with rapid, and sometimes radical, changes.

Throughout this book, my approach to strategy has been shaped more by my work experience than by the literature. My 25-year-long career at General Electric (GE) covered the introduction of strategic planning into the company under the leadership of Reginald H. ("Reg") Jones until its transformation under John F. ("Jack") Welch. This experience gave me an insider's insight into both the benefits and the problems associated with this then new approach to corporate management. Then, for 13 years at SRI International, I had the privilege of working with executives of many global corporations, consulting on strategy and scenario projects in a wide variety of industries and countries. From these experiences I have, I hope, gained a better understanding of what we might call the "strategy culture" that is now an essential element in the corporate makeup.

As an aside, I should note—what will rapidly become apparent to the reader—the frequency with which I cite Welch's leadership in this arena. I should stress that I have *not* set our simply to describe the details of GE and Welch's planning philosophy and practice, for every company must adapt its planning and strategy development system to its own unique needs and culture. However, my familiarity with GE's work has led me to cite their example more frequently than others', and Welch's experience and achievements as chief strategist for GE certainly makes him a persuasive authority to back up my arguments.

Another consequence of my experience has been to focus the contents of this book on the corporate arena. There is ample justification for such a focus, for nowadays nearly all the new thinking and practice in this field has been concentrated in the corporate sphere, and any mention of the term "strategy" seems inevitably to evoke a corporate image. I should point out, however, that the need for strategic thinking, planning, and action is not limited to the corporate world. Rethinking the answers to strategic questions—Who are we? Where are we going? How can we get there?—is a condition for survival of *any* organization in *any* arena where the forces for change are reshaping the number and makeup of the players, the diversity and values of the clients/customers they serve, and the way they serve them. A moment's thought will reveal that these are conditions that apply to, for instance, the fields of education, health care, travel and leisure, community organizations, and even many branches of government. My own experience has led me to work with the United Way, local school systems, hospitals, and charitable organizations on projects that might reasonably be termed "strategic." So, despite the inevitable corporate emphasis in my writing, my hope and aim are that the ideas in this book will speak to and help many others outside the corporate arena.

Finally, a word on the critical importance of strategic *thinking,* rather than strategic *planning.* In the early days of strategic planning, methodology was king: the growth/share matrix, profit impact of market share (PIMS), the experience curve, and other enticing methodologies were on everyone's lips and in everyone's planning books. But while these approaches provided some illuminating insights into portfolio analysis and resource allocation, experience showed that they were sadly deficient when it came to developing innovative strategies.

We can see now that methodologies, in and of themselves, have definite but limited utility. They are needed to provide structure and focus for our thinking, but it is the thinking itself, the creative impulse of the human mind, that provides the ideas and drive for strategy. A central theme for this book, therefore, is that, far more than creating new and improved methodologies, we need to develop in our corporations and other organizations a culture that encourages and requires creative thinking in a blending of strategy and tactics, vision and action, and the future and the present. I explore just what this strategy-oriented culture entails in chapter 7. For the moment it is sufficient to say that this complexity is yet another argument for taking a subtle, rather than a mechanistic, approach to strategy.

Chapter 2

STRATEGIC PLANNING: ITS ORIGINS AND EVOLUTION

"Strategic Planning—It's Back!"
Cover of *Business Week,* August 26, 1996.

It is frustrating and puzzling to me—almost defying logical explanation—to see the wide, sometimes erratic, swings in executives' behavior as they first embrace, and then reject, new approaches to management and planning. If there is one cardinal sin that seems to span national and industry boundaries, it is the apparent belief that there is a single silver bullet for corporate success—a belief that is coupled with rapid shifts in conviction as to what exactly that bullet might be. One would not expect that supposedly rational executives would so easily succumb to the "fad of the month," yet they do. Each year, *Business Week* surveys the shifting scene of management thinking, asking "What's in? what's out?"

Strategic planning has clearly suffered from this vacillating approach. Since its introduction in the early 1970s, it has experienced a roller-coaster ride of stomach-churning proportions. It has been successively a fad, an anathema, and just another management tool. It has bounced around the corporate hierarchy in search of a legitimate role and an appropriate home. Its obsession with a succession of planning methodologies has caused it to oscillate between quantitative and qualitative tools in its analyses, between external and internal emphasis in its situation assessment, and between long-term and short-term focus in its goals and measurements.

No doubt, some of the fault for this erratic behavior has been inherent in strategic planning itself in the course of its evolution from its unsophisticated beginnings to a more coherent approach. Trial and error is a natural part of the process of introducing any new product or way of thinking. But the problem is larger than that. It has been, I am convinced, exacerbated by managers' impatience, their obsession with short-term perspectives, and their failure to grasp the subtle and holistic nature of strategy and the full extent of the changes in thinking, culture, organization, and execution that it entails.

A SHORT HISTORY OF STRATEGIC PLANNING

As a concept and a practice, strategy is as old as Sun Tzu's treatise on "The Art of War" and as new as the latest planning methodology promoted by some consulting firm. But for all except the last 35 years of these more than two millennia, it has been largely confined to the military and geopolitical spheres. Only in the middle to late 1960s did "strategy" become a popular term in the corporate vocabulary and armory.

Looking back over corporate experience and the management literature of this period, we can view the evolution of strategic planning as a drama played out in five (so far) acts.

In Act I, strategic planning enjoyed a heyday of almost unquestioning corporate popularity for nearly a decade—from the late 1960s to roughly 1978—with GE leading the way. Strategic planning was not, of course, unknown before GE introduced its new planning system in 1970–71. Bruce Henderson had founded the Boston Consulting Group in 1963 to focus on thinking about strategy, and Igor Ansoff and Kenneth Andrews had already published seminal volumes on this topic. But, as so often, it was GE's initiative that attracted a great deal of management attention and stimulated considerable corporate action and academic research. Among other things, its actions helped trigger a large, and not always discriminating, "follow-the-leader" movement in the corporate world. By the mid 1970s, no self-respecting chief executive officer would dare appear before the board of directors without a strategic planning system either in place or under development. While at GE, I witnessed the horde of planners and executives who came, notebooks in hand, to review our procedures and training programs, meticulously noting every detail of planning documents and schedules in an effort to transplant our system into their organizations. All too often, they gave little thought to the model's appropriateness to their situation or to the cultural differences involved. Such problems and oversights later came back to haunt many companies.

This period also produced a surge of activity in the consulting field, both in the proliferation of strategic planning boutiques and in the development of a bewildering array of new techniques and methodologies. This was the era of the experience curve, the growth/share matrix, PIMS, and so on. In stripping, Gypsy Rose Lee advised, "You gotta have a gimmick." In planning, the advice appeared to be, "You gotta have a matrix!"

As planning tools proliferated, so too did corporate planning staffs. Unfortunately, the greatest proliferation occurred at the corporate level, even though in most companies the emphasis, so far as strategy development was concerned, was rightly at the strategic business unit (SBU) level. The original impetus for this proliferation came from the time-honored tradition that the emergence of a new function merits the creation of a new staff. Empire building and momentum then set in, and the seeds of an inevitable reaction were sown.

Act II saw the onset of this reaction in the early 1980s. Just as GE had led the way in strategic planning, *Fortune* so led the charge of the critics in a series of articles by Walter Kiechel III. By 1980 growing corporate and academic disenchantment with the results of strategic planning was already apparent, but it was Kiechel's articles—starting with "The Decline of the Experience Curve" and culminating with the cover story, "The Real World Strikes Back: Corporate Strategists under Fire"— that crystallized the revolution.

As Kiechel pointed out, executive disillusionment about strategic planning's results was growing, with much talk of the so-called failed promise. Companies had set up elaborate planning systems and devised sophisticated strategies, but little or nothing had happened. Why? The reasons were many, as we shall see. But whatever the reasons, a routinization of the process further compounded the disenchantment. Executives and staff went through the motions because the system (and the CEO) required them to; they didn't believe in the process, and they ignored its results. This routinization led inevitably to the well-documented implementation problem. In many corporations, strategic planning and operational planning seemed to operate as separate cogs in the corporate mechanism, with little or no visible signs of meshing.

The 1980 and 1982 (especially) recessions struck a further blow to strategic planning. If planning could not foresee these downturns—it was argued—or failed to devise strategies to soften their impacts on the business, what good was it? During this period, disenchantment and cost-reduction measures combined to decimate many corporate planning staffs.

In Act III, in the middle to late 1980s, strategic planning began a tentative comeback in the guise of strategic management. Despite the missteps taken by many corporations in designing their planning systems, the need for strategy and strategic thinking had never been greater. In a seminal article on "The State of Strategic Planning" in *The Economist* in 1987, Michael Porter wrote:

> Strategic planning in most companies has not contributed to strategic thinking. The answer, however, is not to abandon planning. . . . Instead, strategic thinking needs to be rethought and recast. . . . What has been under attack [is] the techniques and organizational processes which companies used. . . .[1]

At least strategic management succeeded in correcting some of the defects of the earlier approach, most notably by placing the main responsibility for strategy in the hands of line managers who are, after all, the ones charged with responsibility for its implementation. Unfortunately, however, this was also the era of corporate raiders, mergers, acquisitions, and financial deal making, and in such a climate, strategic planning could not help being stunted and skewed toward the needs of this singular approach with its nearly exclusive emphasis on short-term profits and defense of the status quo.

Act IV began in the early 1990s with a swing away from long-term strategy toward short-term downsizing to meet the growing globalization of competition. Reengineering and restructuring became the popular mantras of those times. Corporate executives focused mainly on bringing costs under control as economies weakened and new competition invaded their markets in the wake of changes in trade, technology, and regulation. This moved Henry Mintzberg in 1994 to write his book, *The Rise and Fall of Strategic Planning*—although, in a fascinating ambivalence, the *Harvard Business Review* later published an excerpt from the book under the title "The Fall and Rise of Strategic Planning." Which were we supposed to believe? Perhaps these somewhat conflicting titles mirrored the uncertainty, not just of the author and editors, but of the larger business community, as to what their priorities should be and what they might realistically expect of this latest managerial tool. At the time, the need to cut costs, reengineer processes, and restructure basic organization was indeed a strategic imperative, but it left unanswered the larger and ultimate strategic questions: How are our markets changing? What is our growth strategy? On what basis shall we compete? What purposes should our restructuring serve?

Then in 1996, *Business Week* heralded the opening of Act V. "Strategic planning—it's back," the journal proclaimed[2]. "Reengineering consultants with stop-watches are out. Strategy gurus with visions of new prospects are in." And indeed the performance between 1996 and 2002 does seem to offer some hope for a more realistic and sustained, though perhaps less sweeping, role for strategy in the corporate scheme of things.

How should we interpret these oscillations? Do they accurately reflect the history of the past 30 years? No doubt some distortions arise in telling of these events in this way. No doubt, too, the business press, in search of a story, and consultants, in search of new clients, have been guilty of hyping the new and disparaging the old. But, fundamentally, this on-again/off-again approach to strategic planning has been, all too frequently, the way that many corporations have behaved, ignoring the counterproductive consequences of this behavior and the costs of such swings in organization and procedures. I believe that for those who have lived through this period, my summary of these events will strike a chord in their own recollections.

THE IMPERATIVE NEED FOR STRATEGIC THINKING

Before going any further, it is worth pausing to ask ourselves what it was that, around 1965–70, led to the appearance and rapid spread of strategic planning on the management scene in the first place. After all, it is a matter of historical fact that, in corporate behemoths and entrepreneurial enterprises alike, executives had managed to steer their companies successfully for generations without the need to engage in anything as complex and erudite as strategic planning. Yet within the span of five or so short years, the situation had changed radically—not always for the better, as we have seen, but extensively nonetheless.

Once again it is useful to start with a look at GE's experience and reasoning at this juncture. In introducing strategic planning into its management system in 1970, the company cited four driving forces that made a change in the planning system mandatory:

1. *Growing complexity of the organization.* By 1970 GE, which had pioneered decentralization in the 1950s, had more than 150 product departments, many of them the result of a process of division and subdivision, more for the sake of manageability and administrative con-

venience than for market or competitive rationality. It had become imperative to make this growing complexity more manageable; and, to this end, the new planning system was built around a set of 40 or so SBUs, each responsible for managing all aspects of a clearly defined line of products (and services), sold in clearly defined markets, and competing against a clearly defined set of competitors. (It is worth noting that, although this organizational concept was a response to GE's particular needs, it was perhaps the single-most valuable and enduring contribution to other companies' approach to this problem.)

2. *Growing internal competition for resources.* During the 1960s, the company had invested for growth faster than it had generated internal funds and had used debt leverage to the point that, in 1970, its debt had reached an effective limit, consistent with the company's desire to maintain its AAA credit rating. This problem was accentuated by the fact that GE was then trying to nurture three so-called bet-the-company developing businesses—computers, nuclear energy, and aircraft engines—each of which required deep-pocket investments. The new strategic planning system was seen as providing a more rational way of evaluating the long-term prospects for these businesses and for the allocation of corporate resources over the long term. Interestingly, the decision to exit the computer business, taken shortly before the actual introduction of the strategic planning system, remained for several years the best example of strategic analysis and decision making.

3. *Intensifying—and changing—competition.* The breadth and strength of the competition that GE faced was increasing rapidly, partly due to the growing diversity of the company's businesses, but mainly as the result of globalization and industry restructuring. From a strategic point of view, what was new and important about this factor was not so much the increase in intensity of competition, but rather the changes in the character and composition of competitors. Even in 1970 we could see the first signs of the crumbling of boundaries—between countries and economies, among industries, and among technologies—which would lead ultimately to new forms of competition, from new sources, in new markets. Clearly, these incipient changes required a more strategic analysis of industry and market changes and new and different corporate responses.

4. *Rapidly changing business environment.* The five years preceding 1970 had seen the sowing of the seeds of a social and political revolution that was to gain focus and momentum over the next three decades. This was the era of the movements—the anti–Vietnam War movement, the consumer movement, the students' movement, the minority movement, the women's movement, the environmental movement, and the urban renewal movement—to name just a few. Collectively these movements

radically changed the sociopolitical environment in which corporations conducted their business. And their impacts extended beyond the domain of corporate social responsibility and community relations: they directly challenged the legitimacy, the values, and the strategies of major corporations.

Confronted with these four forces, GE concluded that a radical change was needed in its planning, resource allocation, and decision-making systems. Among other things, the company's planning needed to take a much broader look at its markets and (particularly the sources of) competition, to be far more sensitive to new developments in the sociopolitical as well as the economic and technological fields, and, above all perhaps, to be more open to the possibility of radical changes in its environment and correspondingly radical changes in its strategies.

Events of the next decade or so underscored the fundamental soundness of that judgment, not merely for GE, but for almost any large corporation. And, despite the missteps in design and execution of planning systems, the need for strategic planning remained and grew ever stronger. As Porter noted in his 1987 *Economist* article:

> There are no substitutes for strategic thinking. Improving quality is meaningless without knowing what kind of quality is relevant in competitive terms. Nurturing corporate culture is useless unless the culture is aligned with a company's approach to competing. Entrepreneurship unguided by strategic perspective is much more likely to fail than succeed. And, contrary to public opinion, even Japanese companies plan.[3]

Porter's observation was accurate then, it is accurate now; and it is likely to continue to be accurate as far into the future as we can see.

Today, the converging forces of globalization, technology, deregulation, and economic restructuring combine to make strategy and strategic thinking an even more important weapon in the corporate armory. Incremental change in the business environment can generally be dealt with by incremental responses from the corporation. Radical change, however, of the kind that we are now experiencing, requires a radical rethinking of strategic direction and a transformation of capabilities, production, structure, and relationships. This is not exclusively a challenge for high-tech companies. In his book, *Only the Paranoid Survive,* Andy Grove, the chairman of Intel, argues that virtually every industry now confronts a series of "strategic inflection points"—crisis moments when the tectonic plates of the business landscape shift.[4]

Navigating such an environment requires a strategic compass. Strategy cannot be relegated to a backseat or become a sometime practice. It must be a corporate way of life, the equivalent of a corporate gyrocompass, relying on its own inertial guidance system, always seeking the true north, and not allowing other, nearer magnetic fields to dupe or mislead management.

At one level, most managers would agree with these assertions. Who, after all, would want to disagree with the likes of Jack Welch and Michael Porter, Andy Grove and Gary Hamel, all of whom think and act strategically? And indeed the publication of the *Business Week* article and the history of the period from 1996 to 2002 give some hope that this time, maybe, the new corporate commitment to strategic planning might be longer lasting.

And yet. . . . the suspicion persists that executive understanding and support for strategic planning is fragile and will last only until the next economic downturn or the next big thing in management comes along. Sustained commitment will come only from a radical reperceiving of the true nature and role of strategy. Strategy should be holistic in its scope and its approach. It should deal, not with any one particular aspect of the business, but with the business as a whole and its relationship to the business environment as a whole. Strategy derives its power not from an either/or focus on long-term positioning *or* short-term results and product quality *or* process redesign, but rather from a both/and approach and an ability to harness the power of opposites.

WHAT WENT WRONG?

If, then, the case for strategic planning was so strong, why did it fail so miserably in its early years? What went wrong? What was the cause of the so-called failed promise?

I am convinced that at one level a major cause was, as I have already noted, the widespread and too often indiscriminate follow-the-leader movement triggered by GE's initiative. Significantly, the record at GE itself—which understood much better than others the extent of the organizational change involved, and so prepared itself more thoroughly—was smoother and more effective. Certainly, there were mistakes and teething problems, and the whole process underwent a sea change when Jack Welch, took over as CEO in 1981. But the commitment to strategy as a guiding organizational principle remained strong.

More broadly, the fault lay in what I have termed "the seven deadly sins of strategic planning." These were (and still are) the following:

1. *The staff took over the process.* This situation arose partly because CEOs followed tradition and created new staff components to deal with a new function, partly because the staff then moved in to fill a vacuum created by middle management's misunderstanding of, or indifference to, this new responsibility, and partly because of arrogance and empire building. As a result, planning staffs effectively cut executives out of the strategy development process, merely presenting them with strategy options for approval, and ignored the fact that, fundamentally, strategic planning is, and must always be, an executive—not a staff—function. The role of staff should only be that of analyst, organizer, and facilitator of the process, not that of driver nor owner of its results.

2. *The process then came to dominate the staff.* The process's methodologies became increasingly elaborate. Staff placed too much emphasis on analysis and too little on strategic insight. Elaborate studies thus proliferated, impeding decision making and leading to the paralysis by analysis syndrome. Strategic thinking virtually came to be measured by the thickness of the planning books, and documentation became more and more elaborate. In speaking to a group of managers at GE's Crotonville management school, Jack Welch described the resulting situation graphically: "The books got thicker, the printing got more sophisticated, the covers got harder, and the drawings got better." Such a triumph of form over substance is well known to any observer of corporate bureaucracy.

   Paradoxically, however, although the planning process became overly elaborate and bureaucratic, in many cases it came to rely excessively on a single technique or methodology—the experience curve, for instance, or the growth/share matrix. Given the range of issues and factors that strategic planning has to deal with, such reliance was manifestly misplaced. No single methodology could fill all needs, and this approach was doomed to failure.

3. *Planning systems were virtually designed to produce no results.* Perverse though this idea may seem, it was true for many corporate planning systems. The main design failure lay in denying, or diminishing, the planning role of the very executives whose mandate was to execute the strategy. As one critic at the time noted, the attitude of many was typified by the angry retort of one executive, "The matrix picked the strategy—let the matrix implement it!" The other design fault was the failure to integrate the strategic planning system with the operating system, resulting in a disconnect between strategy and action, and so to the notorious implementation problem: great plans—but little to show for them!

4. *Planning focused on the more exciting game of mergers, acquisitions, and divestitures at the expense of core business development.* This prob-

lem stemmed in part from the temper of the times. But it also resulted from the inappropriate use of planning tools such as the growth/share matrix. Above all, it came from a radical misperception about "cash cows." The biggest problem with portfolio planning involved the treatment of these mature businesses. The matrix called for a so-called harvest strategy for these businesses, so companies raised profit goals, curtailed investments, and tightened controls. In due course, not surprisingly, morale in these units dropped, action plans languished, and the business failed to deliver its required cash flow. Even Larry Bossidy, at that time vice chairman of GE, confessed that "We just assumed that, if a business was in a slowly growing market, it was not a very good business. Now we understand much better just how profitable such a business can be, even though its industry is growing by only two percent. Now we have redefined the cash cow concept and are investing a lot of money in SBUs we used to call cash cows."[5]

5. *Planning processes failed to develop true strategic choices.* In their anxiety to prove that they were action oriented, too many companies devised planning systems that fell into the "ready, fire, aim" category. Planners and executives rushed to adopt the first strategy that "satisficed"," that is, that met certain basic conditions in an acceptable manner. They made no real effort to search for, or analyze, an array of strategy alternatives before making a decision. As a result, companies all too often adopted strategies by default rather than by choice.

6. *Strategic planning neglected the organizational and cultural requirements of strategy.* No better example of this exists than the SBU concept. The concept per se is wonderful for identifying and organizing corporate entities appropriate for doing business in defined market segments against a defined set of competitors. However, this focus overlooks or shortchanges the internal differences among SBUs. Thus, the process focused, rightly, on the externalities of the business, but it did so at the expense of the internal environment that is critical in the implementation stages. To its credit, GE foresaw this problem and sought to avert, or at least minimize, it by developing an extensive educational program, which included all executives, would-be strategic planners, and all salaried staff, to introduce not merely the new system, but a new vocabulary and a new way of thinking.

7. *Single-point forecasting was an inappropriate basis for planning in an era of restructuring and uncertainty.* Despite their emphasis on the crucial externalities of the business, and despite the establishment of some sophisticated corporate environmental analysis systems, companies still tended to rely on single-point forecasting. Scenario-based planning was the exception rather than the rule. Unfortunately, in an age of uncertainty, single-point forecasting was—and still is—inher-

ently inaccurate. Plans that relied on it suffered increased vulnerability to surprises, which abounded in the 1970s and early 1980s. Indeed, it was planning's perceived failure to foresee and plan for the sharp recession of 1982 that nearly administered the coup de grâce to strategic planning.

There was a further problem with single-point forecasting. Because planning assumptions spelled out a single future, one that was almost always some slight variation of an extrapolation of past trends, there was an inherent bias in favor of continuing a momentum strategy on the theory that what had worked in the past would probably continue to work in the assumed future. Nothing, unfortunately, could have been further from the truth.

WHAT GOES RIGHT?

With such a record of mistaken approaches and questionable results, it may seem surprising that strategic planning still enjoys any credibility and following in the management community. But we seem to have learned from past experience, not only what can go wrong and doesn't work, but also what works and is worth pursuing.

In a survey of planning practices of nearly 50 global corporations that I conducted in 1996, there was already evidence that they were learning from past mistakes and putting strategic planning on a more balanced and sophisticated basis. Highlights of this survey's findings (see Appendix A for a more detailed reporting) focused on the following points:

- *Changes in emphasis and approach*—There has been a major shift in emphasis in strategic planning toward recognizing the importance of the externalities of the business and the need for more sophisticated executive attention to changing market and competitive conditions. At the same time the balance of responsibility for strategic planning has tilted from staff to line managers and from the corporate level to the SBU level.

- *Challenges to strategic management*—When asked to identify the major challenges that their planning systems were having to deal with, corporations cited the impacts and uncertainties of economic, political, and competitive restructuring as the primary external challenges. Internally, the overwhelming challenge, which was cited by virtually every respondent, was the need to change the cultural and organizational traits that impede effective strategic management: risk aversion, short-term perspectives, lack of executive vision, bureaucratic inertia and inflexibility, turf concerns, size, and poor communications. Other challenges included financial problems (cost control and the need to improve portfolio management), operational problems (the need to improve the linkage between tactics and strategy, between production and marketing, between research and development [R&D] and operations), and the pressure to stay abreast of technological change.

- *Perceived benefits of strategic planning (management)*—The three most highly rated benefits were (1) a clearer sense of strategic vision; (2) a sharper focus, in planning and execution, on strategically important issues; and (3) improved understanding of the rapidly changing business environment. The survey responses made clear that companies had high hopes for strategic management but recognized that they had yet to realize these benefits fully.

- *The role of corporate planning units*—Despite the decentralization of planning to business units, companies continued to maintain a strategic planning capability at the corporate level to focus on companywide strategic issues, to develop overall corporate strategy (such as portfolio investment priorities), and to draft guidelines for executive approval to help SBUs develop their strategies.

- *The use of methodologies*—Despite the continuing lure of fads, most corporate strategic planning units were moving toward reduced reliance on a single silver bullet methodology. Indeed, the survey results suggested that most companies use, on average, four key methodologies in their process, with core competencies, scenario planning, and benchmarking being cited most frequently.

Since that survey, the learning process has continued. We have learned, for instance, that strategy is a continuous, ongoing process. We can no more fit it neatly into a planning calendar, or circumscribe it with textbook procedures, than we can halt the changes in the environment that we seek to understand. What we need, far more than a new methodology, is an organizational culture that encourages us to think and act strategically.

We cannot escape strategy, so we had better get good at it.

The first, and most important, lesson that the experience of the past 30 years should have taught us is that it is strategic *thinking,* rather than strategic planning per se, that should be our goal. I recognize that this may seem to some to be nothing more than yet another consultant's semantic quibble. In an arena in which we have seen many efforts to define differences where there were little or none—attempts to distinguish core capabilities from core competencies, for example, or to single out time-to-market or value-chain analysis as *the* key to competitive advantage—we should rightly be skeptical of attempts to focus on a single feature as the true essence of strategy. We can, however, surely agree that dynamic ideas and concepts (which are the product of thinking) differ from, and are more important than, process, methodologies, and numbers (which are the product of by-the-book planning). Strategy clearly needs dynamic ideas as its driving force: process and methodology are merely a structured way (but not the only way) of arriving at these ideas.

The notion of strategic thinking has the further advantage of bridging the divide between plan and action. Planning ends with the development of the plan, but strategy is nothing if it is not carried forward into action. And it is thinking—the development of concepts in the plan and the ability to think quickly, to adapt the plan to changing circumstances—that links planning and action and ensures consistency and that is the heart and driver of strategy.

The second lesson that we should have learned is that *executives' ownership* of the strategy development process—not merely their pro forma involvement in it—is essential if the resulting strategy is to have any chance of being translated into action, let alone success. "The CEO (or SBU manager) should be her own planner" is now a widely accepted maxim. Executives cannot be fully committed to implementing a plan unless they have played so strong a role in developing it that the plan has become *their* idea. This truth suggests the desirability of an executive team, rather than the CEO alone, being involved in strategy development.

What clearly must follow from this new emphasis on executive ownership is a redefinition of the role of the planner (and the consultant). No longer should planners be the architects of strategy. They can, and should, orchestrate the process, help catalyze the development of ideas, supply the necessary strategic analyses, monitor the results (and the changing environment), and develop the planning calendar. But they must not usurp the executive prerogative.

Third, we have learned—or, by now, should have—the imperative of facing up to, and dealing constructively with, uncertainty that is woven inextricably and pervasively throughout the tapestry of the business environment. The pioneering work of Royal Dutch/Shell on scenario planning has shown both how necessary and how difficult this lesson is to execute, for it challenges some of the basic premises of the traditional corporate planning culture. It is only a slight exaggeration to say that, in most corporations, planning is essentially conceived as an exercise in reducing, and if possible, eliminating, uncertainty. Its underlying premise is, "Forecast the future, then plan for it." This belief is reinforced by a conviction that links management with knowledge: good managers *know* where they are, *know* where they are going, and *know* how they will get there. In such a culture, acknowledging uncertainty is equivalent to a confession of not-knowing, an admission that no manager wants to make.

But we have learned, to our cost, that we cannot forecast the future and that strategies that are based on single-point forecasting are highly vulnerable. Difficult though it may be, we really have no option but to face up to, and deal with, the inevitable uncertainties that will confront whatever strategy we adopt.

The fourth lesson is that successful strategy development requires both an outside-in and an inside-out perspective on the business. Companies need to develop both a sensitivity to current and impending changes in their market and industry (and to what these changes mean for the business) and a clear-eyed, hardheaded analysis of their own strengths and weaknesses. Furthermore, strategy development should allow and indeed encourage iterations of these converging perspectives. This goes against the grain of our training in which linear progression seems to dominate our thinking (and our schematic representations of planning systems). We move from one step to another, from the left-hand side of the chart to the right, in a steady, logical progression toward the plan. This lack of iteration overlooks the insights that an interplay between environmental and competitive analysis, on the one hand, and capabilities analysis, on the other, can reveal. Encouraging iteration means, for instance, that instead of merely identifying strengths and weaknesses by its own standards (asking, for instance, "What are we good at?"—and then, in effect, replying "Practically everything"!), a corporation must make a truer assessment of its real competitive position by using the standards of its competition and customers in light of the changing market needs. A corporation must assess the areas in which it has a *sustainable* competitive advantage and then realize that its true strengths are far more limited.

Finally, we have discovered the critical importance of having a supportive organizational culture that actively nurtures strategic thinking. As we have already noted, strategic thinking is far more than methodology. It is the product of critical analysis, imagination, intuition, risk taking, vision, and flexibility. These are qualities that cannot flourish in the typical hierarchical and restrictive climate in most corporations. But they are essential if we are to be truly strategic in our orientation and our performance. So we are, in effect, confronted with a double challenge: we must develop and execute the right strategy and at the same time create both the organization structure and climate in which that strategy can evolve.

Building on these lessons, we can move more easily to explore, in the following chapters, the critical precepts that underlie what I term "the subtle art of strategy." There can be little argument with the notion that strategy is far more of an art form than a science or craft. If that were not so—if, for instance, we could develop and execute strategy by some set formula—there would be far more first-class strategists: every CEO could be a Jack Welch or Jorma Ollila.[6] But then there would be virtual corporate stalemate, with no clear winners or losers, as one perfect strategy battled with others.

The truth, however, is that there is no easy, cut-and-dried formula, there are only helpful methodologies—and these give only part of the answer. Strategy is a blend of the pragmatic and the ideal, the intuitive and the analytical, the internal and the external, and the long-term and the short-term. And this is a blending that only the individual human mind, with its capacity for dealing with complexity and subtlety, can achieve.

NOTES

1. Michael E. Porter, "Corporate Strategy: The State of Strategic Thinking," *The Economist*, 23 May 1987.

2. Ibid.

3. Andrew Grove, *Only the Paranoid Survive* (New York: Currency/Doubleday, 1996).

4. Andy Grove, *Only the Paranoid Survive.*

5. Lawrence A. Bossidy, "Some Thoughts on Strategic Thinking" (speech presented to the Strategic Management Society, Boston, 14 October 1987).

6. John F. Welch Jr., chairman and chief executive officer of GE (1981–2001) in the United States; and Jorma Ollila, chairman and CEO of Nokia in Finland.

Chapter 3

THE MANY FACES OF STRATEGY

"When *I* use a word," Humpty Dumpty said, in rather a scornful tone,
"it means just what I chose it to mean—neither more nor less."
                    Lewis Carroll, *Alice's Adventures in Wonderland*

WHAT *IS* STRATEGY?

This question would seem to be a reasonable starting point for our quest into the nature of strategic thinking and action. However, no sooner have we raised the question than are we confronted with a bewildering array of answers. Nowadays strategy is in, and everyone—corporations, consultants, hospitals, schools, community planning groups, even churches and the United Way[1]—seems to want a piece of the action. No one wants to be left out of what is now considered an essential planning tool for any self-respecting organization.

This might be fine, if only everyone could agree on what we are talking about: but we can't. Read any collection of annual reports, and you will see what I mean. Strategy is defined in a wide variety of ways—as an aspiration (". . . to be the predominant supplier in our chosen markets"), as a financial objective (". . . to earn 15 percent return on investment"), as an operating principle (". . . to leverage our technological strengths in the development of cutting-edge products"), as an organizational arrangement (". . . to build a global network of strategic alliances to serve the XYZ market").

But the problem is not only of corporations' making. For a wide variety of motives—from a bona fide effort to clarify the picture to a less commendable desire to develop a distinctive signature theory—educators and consultants have contributed to a bewildering proliferation of definitions. In their book, *Strategy Safari: A Guided Tour through the Wilds of Strategic Management,* Henry Mintzberg and his coauthors, Bruce Ahlstrand and Joseph Lampel, identified no fewer than 10 major schools of thought, from the Design School, to the Planning School and the Learning School, to the Configuration School. We are all like blind men, they assert, and strategy is our elephant: everyone has seized some part or other of the animal and ignored the rest (see Appendix B).

As an alternative, we might turn to a dictionary for a resolution of our problem. Unfortunately, however, these definitions, while logical and commendably precise, are still shaded by the military connotations that have historically been associated with strategy. For instance, *Webster's* gives us this definition of the term:

> *Strategy:* The science of planning and directing large-scale military operations, specifically (as distinguished from tactics) of maneuvering forces into the most advantageous position prior to actual engagement with the enemy.[2]

This is a useful starting point and, with a little imagination, we might adapt this terminology to the corporate setting while keeping as close as possible to the original wording: "Strategy is the science [or art?] of planning and managing a corporation's operations, specifically (as distinguished from tactics) of positioning a corporation in its chosen markets to achieve maximum sustainable advantage over its competitors."

However, this definition also underscores some of the ways in which strategy in the military arena differs significantly from its corporate counterpart. For one thing, the two forms of strategy deal with different time frames: in the military sphere, the emphasis is on the near-term and the prospect of a conclusion to the operation, whereas the corporate strategist is confronted with a continually evolving and receding horizon. Then, too, there are differences in the territory that each covers—the stable, physical topography, in the case of military operations, and the changing flux of markets and competition, in corporate strategy. Further, military strategy is normally directed against a singular enemy, but corporate strategy has to deal with multiple enemies (i.e., competitors) with widely differing interests, territories, and capabilities. Finally, there is a deep-seated cultural difference: the primary qualities sought in the military are order and discipline, while in the corporate sphere they are innovation and entrepreneurial flexibility. These and other differences lead us to the inexorable conclusion that the military has only limited value as a model for designing strategy in a corporate setting.

However, the dictionary definition—or something close to it—does begin to capture, in a few words, something of the essence of strategy. Indeed, if we amplify it with the phrasing that Jack Welch once used to convey his own sense of what is meant by the term "strategy," we come close to our goal. Speaking informally to a group of MBA students at the Harvard Business School, Welch explained:

> Strategy is trying to understand where you sit today in today's world. Not where you wish you were and where you hoped you would be, but where you are. And [it's trying to understand] where you want to be . . . [It's] assessing with everything in your head the competitive changes that you can capitalize on or ward off to go from here to there. It's assessing the realistic chances of getting from here to there.[3]

This is clearly a definition-in-use rather than a dictionary definition, but it conveys graphically both the activities and the state of mind that are involved in strategic thinking. The thought and the phrasing are pure Welch, combining passion and logic, eliminating the professional gobbledygook, and reducing the abstract to down-to-earth terms that any manager could understand.

However, at the risk of sounding like Humpty Dumpty, I want to offer my own briefer, but (I believe) still accurate, definition of strategy that can then be unfolded into an elaboration of its ramifications and implications. In my view:

> Strategy is the driving force that shapes the future nature and direction of the business. It defines the corporate vision and the means that will be employed to achieve that vision.

By "means," I intend to include the whole panoply of resources available to the business and the substrategies it employs in pursuit of its goals— for instance, the business's positioning in its markets, the basis on which it will compete, its technology thrusts, organization and human resources strategy, and alliances and joint ventures.

Before proceeding any further, I should point out that this matter of definition is no mere semantic quibble. It is important, for several reasons, not least to distinguish strategy from statements of mission, values, and vision—all of which have a valuable, but differing, role to play. Mission, for example, sets out the basic purpose of the business, defines the arena in which it will operate and the customers it will serve, and sets broad objectives for the business. A values statement, on the other hand, articulates the corporate values that will be the guiding principles for corporate actions and ethical behavior, defines the character of its relations with stakeholders, and establishes management style and corporate culture. And strategic vision describes the shape of the future business, sets specific goals, and drives strategy. (For a fuller glossary of terms used in strategic planning, see Appendix C.)

Each of these statements has an essential role to play in defining corporate direction, culture, and actions. Each, therefore, needs to be widely communicated and understood, creating a shared sense of purpose throughout the organization. But that will occur only if we are clear about the meaning of the terms and are persuaded that they are to be taken seriously rather than viewed as public relations trappings.

ATTRIBUTES OF STRATEGIC THINKING

Thinking, rather than fact finding, is the critical dynamic of strategy, both in its conception and in its execution. Facts are, of course, a necessity, but no amount of fact gathering and analysis alone can take the place of intuition, insight, or the entrepreneurial hunch. What is needed for truly strategic thinking is a blending of unusual qualities. It is thinking that is holistic, focused, visionary, inquisitive, flexible, and decisive.

Holistic

Strategic thinking is holistic in the sense that it takes a comprehensive view of the business—the *totality* of its functions, interests, and operations in the context of its *total* environment (markets, competitive, economic, technological, and sociopolitical). Only by taking this broad perspective is it possible to determine the strategic moves required to adjust to—or, better yet, to help shape—the dynamic forces that are reshaping this environment.

Consider, for example Dell Computer's new business model strategy. This is truly a holistic approach to business strategy involving as it does a combination of the following:

- A customer relations strategy of dealing directly with customers, rather than through a distribution chain
- A manufacturing strategy of custom manufacturing to order, rather than for inventory

- A supplier relations strategy of integrating suppliers' and Dell's own processes into a virtually seamless just-in-time throughput process
- A technology strategy that enables the close integration of customers, manufacturer, supplier, and dispatcher

Focused

Although strategic thinking is holistic in its scope, it is also, from another perspective, intensely focused, in two senses. First, it is focused on identifying and then resolving the key strategic issues arising out of the impact of the changing environment on the business. These are the truly critical, make-or-break issues for the business; and, in my experience, there are typically only a handful—say, four to six—of such issues at any given time.[4] Second, the thinking is focused on a single product: the development and elaboration of a business strategy. It is only by being so focused, rather than letting itself be diverted into resolving a multitude of operational issues, that strategic thinking can become the true driver of the business.

Visionary

In this context, vision is not the soft, indefinable, intangible term that most of us think of when we hear this word. As I argue in chapter 5 ("The Power of Strategic Vision"), it is hard, specific, practical, and indeed essential, in a strategic context. Vision is "a coherent and powerful statement of what the business can, and should, be (10) years hence" (the time frame varies with the nature of the business). It is an embodiment and expression of the strategy and the results that pursuing that strategy can achieve. At its best, therefore, it is a vital element in communicating the strategy, an expression of shared purpose, and a powerful motivator of individual and group performance.

Practical

Along with its visionary quality, strategic thinking must also have a highly practical bent. This is so because the ultimate goal is, of course, not just a strategic plan, but strategic *action* to achieve the vision. Strategic thinking is, therefore, inexorably bound up with implementation, the rock on which early attempts at strategic planning foundered. It must, therefore, always ask, at every stage of strategy development, "Is it realistic? Is it doable? Does it fit with our capabilities?"

Inquisitive/Probing

Strategic thinking should also be profoundly questioning of just about everything—about the corporation's self-assessment (its true strengths and weaknesses), about market forecasts and the reasoning behind them, about the adequacy of its competitive intelligence, and even—and most especially—about its own strategy. Too often a company will adopt the first strategy that (to use the old Scottish term) "satisfices," that is, meets certain minimal conditions. More often than not, this is a business as usual strategy or some slight modification of the current course, because that is what suits the comfort level of management practice. It is almost certain to fall far short of meeting new challenges or adopting new approaches.

It is not too much to say that true strategic thinking requires a range of strategic options to be developed and evaluated before one is finally selected. Development of these strategic options can make the difference between mediocrity and excellence in strategic thinking. Without new options, the process is largely a waste of time. Further, the options must be more than straw men designed to pay lip service to this requirement without changing the substance. Some of these options should be constructed to push the envelope of possibilities so that, by the time the final selection is made, the full range of options open to the business will have been canvassed and evaluated. It is in this sense that strategic thinking needs to be inquisitive, ever-questioning, probing for new insights, and exploring new possibilities.

Flexible

In conditions of extreme uncertainty, strategy must, of necessity, be flexible, capable of adapting rapidly to the unforeseen. This flies in the face of traditional management thinking with its emphasis on hierarchical decision making, fixed planning schedules, and lock step adherence to the so-called plan. These qualities might have been appropriate in an era of greater predictability than we now enjoy; but they are the kiss of death in the age of uncertainty. We know now that we cannot predict even the limited future with any degree of accuracy, but we also know that we cannot meet the future unprepared. So planning is still necessary, but it is planning of a different order. It is planning on a virtually continuous basis, not part of a fixed calendar; planning that is inextricably interwoven with implementation, assessment, and adjustment; planning that is flexible in its execution but still operating within a set of goals and prescribed guidelines.

Decisive

It may seem superfluous to stipulate this quality, which is normally assumed to be a sine qua non of good management. But the ever-present threat of paralysis by analysis and the memory of the failed promise of strategic planning in the 1970s are still with us. So we would do well to restate the obvious: the objective of strategic thinking is not the plan, but the actions that this thinking sets in motion. So thinking must be action oriented at all times.

Holistic, focused, visionary, practical, probing, flexible, decisive— these are the essential attributes of strategic thinking. I realize that this grouping of qualities may seem to be exaggerated, even idealistic, and possibly unattainable. Yet this is precisely why strategy, and strategic thinking, is so difficult: if it is a subtle art, it is also a hard taskmaster.

ATTRIBUTES OF THE STRATEGIC PLAN

It is often said that planning (the act of thinking through the basis on which we will compete) is more important than the plan. I would agree, but that is not to say that the plan itself is unimportant. It is not an end in itself, as we may have originally thought, but it plays an important role as an encapsulation of our thinking, a sketch map of our future moves, and a communications tool. It is important, therefore, that we get it right.

Strategic planning can occur on at least two levels—corporate or SBU. At the corporate level, the focus is on managing a balanced portfolio of profitable, growing businesses that adds value to shareowner investment. Here the primary concerns include the following:

- Identifying and acting on companywide strategic issues
- Deploying and redeploying assets within the company's portfolio
- Exploiting synergies across business units
- Entering major new areas (outside the charter of existing business units)
- Reshaping and renewing the corporation (structure and culture)
- Increasing the value of shareowner investment
- Providing guidelines to help business units develop their strategies.

At the business unit level, the focus is on developing and executing an integrated business strategy that exploits competitive advantage in selected market areas. Here the primary strategic concerns include the following:

- Anticipating and meeting the changing needs of customers in selected market areas
- Determining the key success factors for the business and the strategic basis on which it will compete
- Developing new products and services and seeking to compress the "time to market"
- Improving the productive use of all resources (personnel management, materials, capital, technology, and time)
- Seeking to extend the profitable reach of the business unit through strategic alliances, joint ventures, cross-licensing, and other measures

The principal mistake that many strategic plans make is overkill, that is, including in their analyses and conclusions just about everything that could be said about the business, its markets, and competition, and then overlaying that with endless pages of financial projections (the dollar sign being taken as evidence of certainty!). In the process any vestige of strategic thinking that may have been present is lost in this traditional labyrinth of corporate planning.

I had occasion to allude to this failing a number of years ago when I was lecturing at my corporate alma mater, GE's Management Development Institute in Crotonville, New York, At the end of my presentation I was asked what I *really* thought, now that I had left the company, of GE's vaunted strategic planning system. After detailing my criticism of what I felt was overly bureaucratic and burdensome documentation that cloaked rather than highlighted any vestige of strategic thinking, I concluded that, in my opinion, "A truly strategic (as opposed to operational) plan can be presented in some 20 or so pages." At this point a voice came from the back of the class saying, "I would say, rather, a half dozen pages—followed by three hours of discussion!" The voice was that of Jack Welch, who had just arrived to give his version of a commencement address to this class.

This was a point of view that Welch carried into action in redesigning the company's planning system. By 1986, five years after taking over as CEO, he had radically changed the business planning review process by asking each business to prepare one-page answers to five key questions:

1. What are your market dynamics globally today, and where are they going over the next several years?
2. What actions have your competitors taken in the last three years to upset those global dynamics?
3. What have you done in the last three years to affect those dynamics?

4. What are the most dangerous things your competitors could do in the next three years to upset those dynamics?

5. What are the most effective things you could do to bring your desired impact on these dynamics?

These responses then formed the basis for a tightly focused and grueling discussion led by Welch, and pity the poor SBU manager who wilted under this relentless give-and-take, who didn't have simple, straightforward answers, or who tried to mask the absence of ideas with complex formulas or trite, by-the-book strategies.

Most companies, I know, would not be comfortable with such a curtailed and focused process: the written word and detailed analyses and financial projections are still the essence of most planning systems. And most CEOs rely too much on staff work to be able to wing it on their own in strategy review sessions or are too reluctant to challenge the ideas served up to them by subordinates who were once their peers and colleagues.

All of this is not to deny the usefulness, indeed the necessity, of having a formal planning document. It is, rather, to suggest that the best way of developing a dynamic and resilient strategy is through greater reliance on thinking and the interplay of ideas and viewpoints rather than on sterile analyses. It is also to suggest that, in developing the actual planning document, less is best: keep the emphasis on the truly strategic, and leave the operational details and the financial projections to a separate document.

While the exact format and content of such a document should be tailored to the particular needs and management style of each organization, the following outline shows how a typical planning document might build upon three main components:

- Summary of the strategy
- Rationale for the strategy
- Translating the strategy into action.

1. Summary of the Strategy
   The first three sections of the strategic plan are intended to highlight the essentials of the strategy. For instance:

   A. Strategic vision
      A summary of the longer-term (e.g., more than 5 years) aspirations and objectives of the organization

B. Proposed strategy
Highlights of the strategy for achieving the vision, including details
of the business's market and competitive positioning moves, proposed portfolio changes, acquisitions/alliances, and so forth

C. Near-term goals
Specific goals, both quantitative and qualitative, that should be
achieved over the next one to three years as steps toward longer-
term objectives

2. Rationale for the strategy
Two sections present the rationale for the proposed strategy:

A. Environmental assumptions
The major assumptions underlying the vision/strategy with respect
to:

- Macro trends/events (domestic and international)—developments
  in the broad social, political, economic, and technological environment likely to affect the business

- Micro trends/events —critical dynamics of the business's key markets and competition

- Critical uncertainties in these assumptions/forecasts

Note: Scenarios, if any, would be discussed here.

B. Strategic issues and options
Discussion of the key strategic issues confronting the business, arising from the impact of environmental forces on the organization's
current position (including its strengths and weaknesses)
Review of the strategy options considered and selected/rejected (including the pros and cons of each option)

3. Translating the strategy into action
Three sections detail the action/resources/financial implications involved in translating the proposed strategy into action:

A. Implementation plans
Specific plans/projects for the next one to three years designed to
translate the strategy into action (marketing, production, distribution,
R&D, licensing, human resources, organization, etc.)
Specifying, for each project, responsibilities, schedules, resource re-
quirements (capital, human resources, technology, etc.)

B. Financial implications
Forecast financial results of implementing the strategy (sales, costs,
profit, market shares, etc.), year by year for the next three years
Capital budget required, year by year for the next three years

C. Contingency plans

   Summary of plans (responsibilities, proposed actions, trigger points, impacts) to deal with major contingencies

ATTRIBUTES OF STRATEGIC MANAGEMENT

There are substantial differences, beyond that of nomenclature, between strategic planning as it was practiced in the 1970s and strategic management as it has emerged since the early 1990s or so. To begin with, strategic management has more to do with actually running the business and less to do with developing a pro forma plan. Strategic management can best be defined as running the business on the basis of a coherent vision of what the business can and should be, guided by two key principles: (1) Positioning the business for long-term competitive advantage in a continuously changing business environment; and (2) using strategy (and a strategic management process) to drive decision making at all levels of the organization.

In fact, at the risk of pushing the reader's tolerance beyond the breaking point, I would opt for the phrase "integrated strategic management" as most descriptive of current best practices in corporate strategic planning. In this phrase, each word carries special significance.

- Thus, the term is intended to describe a system that integrates thinking, planning, and management; links planning to operational implementation; integrates functional strategies into a coherent strategy for the business as a whole; and embraces both long-term and short-term perspectives.

- The system is strategic because it focuses attention on the critical issues that must be resolved to ensure optimum competitive and market positioning; it uses strategy to drive decision making at all levels of the organization; and it seeks to diffuse strategic thinking throughout the organization.

- And, finally, the term "management" is intended to emphasize that this process aims to run the business as a continuous iteration of planning, decision making, resource allocation, and execution; it recognizes the critical importance of organizational structure and culture; and it underscores the central role of executives (versus staff) in the process.

Although the details and sequence of the strategic management process varies (as it should) from company to company, Figure 3.1 illustrates 10 steps that most companies incorporate into their systems. A brief description of these steps follows.

Figure 3.1
The Flow of Strategic Management

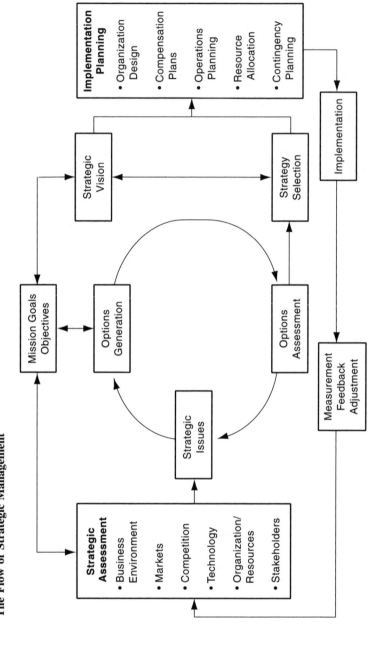

1. Conceptually at least, the process starts with a strategic assessment of the current and future situation in which the business finds itself. This covers trends in the economic, social, and political environment; market developments and changing customer needs; existing and prospective competitors and their strategies; and developments in old and emerging technologies. Internally, this assessment should take a realistic, clear-eyed view of the business's ability to respond effectively to these trends, paying particular attention to rating its own resources and capabilities against those of its competitors. Typically, this assessment culminates in what is known as a SW/OTs analysis—the critical strengths and weaknesses of the business in dealing with the opportunities and threats of the business environment.

2. This comprehensive assessment leads to focusing on the key strategic issues confronting the business. As I have already mentioned, these are the truly critical make-or-break issues that the business must resolve if it is to succeed and prosper in the new environment.

3. The whole strategy development process is played out against a backdrop of the existing statements of mission, goals, and objectives. As indicated in the schematic chart, there will necessarily be an interaction between these statements and the evolving strategic options (and the final strategy), as a result of which there will likely be some modification of these goals and objectives (and even of the corporate mission, in the event of some radical change in strategic direction).

4. The actual strategy development process starts with identification of the fullest possible range of plausible options that the business might pursue. At this stage, the emphasis should be on pushing the envelope of proactive ideas as to how the company might best respond to the challenges posed by the strategic issues, including (most especially) those options that challenge conventional wisdom, for it is there that the greatest competitive advantage may reside. Strategy should be, as I have said, a matter of choice, and the choice will be limited unless novel, unconventional ideas are advanced and considered seriously, not viewed simply as straw men or token options.

5. Assessment of these options follows next. It helps executives to develop out-of-the-box ideas for strategy options if they know that the options will be subject to a rigorous assessment process. Otherwise they might hesitate to bring forward novel ideas for fear that they might be accepted or rejected too quickly. At this stage we need to give careful thought to selecting the criteria to be used in this assessment to ensure that each option is evaluated from a variety of perspectives. It is not enough, for example, to project the relative market size and growth rate, the degree of competition, and profit potential

for each option. It is also important to assess such factors as How much of a stretch would each option present to the company? What is its degree of risk? How much of a competitive advantage does the company bring to pursuit of each option? Here, as so often in strategy, it is the qualitative as much as the quantitative, the judgmental as much as the analytical, that counts. More often than not it is useful, or even necessary, to repeat the issues, or options, assessment cycle to provide an opportunity for second thoughts and additional ideas in light of this first pass at generating strategic options.

6. This assessment then leads to strategy selection—the moment of truth in this whole process. Although it is possible to quantify the assessment of options against the criteria, and then to total up the scores and declare a winner, the selection is, once again, more often a matter of judgment, whether of the executive team or of the CEO. The selected strategy should then be played against the strategic vision.

7. The strategic vision (if it already exists; if not, a vision statement should be developed) should be examined to ensure consistency with the selected strategy or to pinpoint the need for any changes in the vision or the strategy. (See chapter 5 for a detailed description of the nature and role of strategic vision).

8. At this point the strategy can be translated into specific implementation plans for the various components and functions of the company. This is the critical juncture between strategy and operations, the point at which detailed goals, action plans, responsibilities, and financial projections can be developed. In addition to the functional strategies (e.g., marketing, production, distribution, human resources, technology/R&D), this planning should also cover organization design (including the need for strategic alliances), capital investment and resource allocation, and—critical in these uncertain times—contingency planning.

9. Moving from strategy to planning implementation—one of the fatal flaws of strategic planning in the 1970s—focuses on the execution of these operational plans. Here strategy and its execution are driven down deep into the organization, emphasizing once again the need for persistent communication of the strategy so that those charged with its execution are thoroughly conversant with its details, are committed to it, and can execute it as their own.

10. Finally, the strategy loop is closed with measurement of results, continuous feedback into the planning system, and adjustments to the strategy as required by corporate performance or as changes in the external business environment dictate.

Any schematic diagram such as this has some artificiality about it and so should be viewed with a certain degree of caution. However, it does draw our attention to three features that are noteworthy because we should treat them literally, not just figuratively.

First, it is more than design convenience that places the elements that set the overall strategic direction of an organization—mission, goals, objectives, and vision—on an upper level in the schematic. They are, indeed, the overarching principles that shape both the process and the strategy. They are, too, the clearest expression of management values in a process that tends, otherwise, to emphasize analysis and objectivity. Unfortunately, most executives are uncomfortable dealing explicitly with value-laden statements (not recognizing that nearly all their judgments fall into this category) and so tend to curtail, or even trivialize, action on these elements, particularly on mission and vision.

The second noteworthy feature is the centrality, and circularity, of the options phase. As I have emphasized, strategy should be a matter of choice, selecting from a range of possible options. So generating and assessing the alternative strategies among which executives must choose is the creative heart of the system. This phase is also iterative, because the right choice is seldom apparent immediately. More frequently, the initial alternatives fail to satisfy the selection criteria fully but do help to generate new options for examination, elaboration, and assessment. The process takes time, but the time is well spent if it generates a drive toward a new competitive strategy.

Third, this strategic management process is a closed-loop system. The schematic suggests, correctly, that strategic management is a continuous learning experience, a cybernetic system with built-in feedback and constant adjustment. In this respect, it differs from the model of the 1970s, which had more in common with a linear throughput system: Planning led to strategy, which led (ideally) to action, in a series of discrete steps. As in technology development, continuous incremental improvement in strategy can sometimes achieve gains as great as those that result from major breakthroughs.

All this may strike some executives as a great deal of effort for very little in the way of improved results. After all, the history of the past 20 years is replete with examples of corporate stumbling or failure—long before the technology-led collapse of 2000–2001—even among those that claimed to have good planning systems. The cases of companies as diverse as General Motors, IBM, Sears, Aetna, Westinghouse, Motorola, Lucent Technologies, and Campbell Soup readily come to mind, all one-time industry leaders. If strategic planning did not help even these titans, it might be argued, why bother with it? Indeed, the danger with citing any example of good corporate practice these days is that, three years later, it is likely to seem to be a laughable fiasco.

With all that said, however, I strongly believe, with Michael Porter, that the need for strategic thinking has never been greater. And the respondents to my survey (see Appendix A) seemed to agree, feeling that there is much to be gained from having a good strategic management system, most notably a clearer sense of vision, a sharper focus in strategy and operations, and improved understanding of the business environment. Elaborating somewhat on their responses, I would argue, that properly conceived and executed, such a system can develop through the following:

- Understanding of the dynamics of the company's business environment, preparation for change, and reduced vulnerability to surprises (through the thoroughness of macroenvironmental analysis and the use of scenarios)

- Imaginative and profitable market/competitive positioning of the business (through strategic analyses and the development of creative options)

- Focused attention—and action—on the resolution of key strategic make-or-break issues

- Treatment of strategy as informed and creative choice rather than sheer momentum (through developing a range of strategy options)

- Strategy that is flexible and resilient enough to succeed in diverse conditions (through the use of scenarios, consideration of options, and the development of contingency plans)

- A clear and driving sense of corporate purpose and direction (through developing a shared vision of the future business)

- Commitment to implementing the strategy and close integration of strategy and operations (through using executives to drive the strategic decision-making process)

- Widespread diffusion of strategic thinking throughout the organization (though communicating the vision and developing a strategic culture)

In sum, there are four quintessential qualities—the "four I's"—that are the hallmark of good strategic management thinking: insight, intent, innovation, and implementation (see Figure 3.2). Relating these qualities to the 10-step process that I have just outlined, we can see the following:

- Insight derives from focused strategic analyses and the identification of key issues that the strategy must address. These exercises aim for a qualitative breakthrough in strategic insight—achieving the "Aha!" experience that leads to an innovative strategy

Figure 3.2
The Qualities of Strategic Thinking

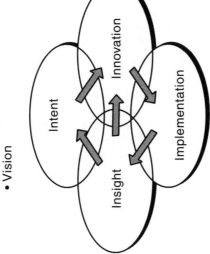

Commitment through:
- Mission
- Goals/Objectives
- Vision

Clarity in:
- Strategic Analyses
- Issues Identification

Creativity in:
- Options Generation
- Strategy Selection
- Organization Design
- Implementation Planning

Consistency in :
- Execution
- Measurement
- Feedback/Adjustment

Intent

Innovation

Insight

Implementation

- Intent—the clarification and communication of the organization's direction and vision—develops out of statements of mission, goals and objectives, and vision that are sufficiently clear and well communicated to engage the commitment of executives, managers, and employees—and, indeed, other stakeholders

- Innovation is the product of a constant emphasis on creativity in thinking through the implications of strategic issues, generating a challenging set of options, and designing plans, programs, organization structure, and culture to give expression to the strategic vision.

- Implementation —made up of execution, measurement, feedback, and adjustment—forges consistent links between planning and action and ensures that strategy drives operational decision making throughout the organization.

NOTES

1. See, for instance, Marvin W. Petersen, David D. Dill, Lisa A. Mets, and associates, eds., *Planning and Management for a Changing Environment* (San Francisco: Jossey-Bass, 1997).

2. Taken from *Webster's New 20th Century Dictionary,* 2d. ed. (1973).

3. "The New Breed of Strategic Planner," *Business Week,* 17 September 1984.

4. This is not to say that there are only a few issues that confront a business at any given time. Indeed, the sum total of all the functional and operational issues that a business has to deal with simultaneously may be in the hundreds. However, only a handful of this total have the potential for making or breaking the business strategically.

Chapter 4

HARNESSING THE POWER OF OPPOSITES

Nothing more emphasizes the complexity and subtlety of strategy than the fact that it is, and must be, multidimensional, holistic in its approach to the business and all its stakeholders, and pervasive in its impact on every aspect and function of the company. Tying strategic planning to any one aspect of competitive success—even one as worthy and unexceptional as growth—sets it up for yet another fall. In an issue that highlighted the return of strategic planning (August 26, 1996), *Business Week* editorialized that "the biggest benefit of strategic planning is its emphasis on growth." I disagree. If growth is not the issue, or if a company meets its growth targets, then in this view strategic planning is no longer necessary.

In my view, the greatest benefit of strategic planning is that it encourages, indeed forces, managers to take a holistic view of the business and of the economic, social and political setting on which it operates. It requires that we look at, deal with, and develop strategies for every aspect, every function, and every stakeholder of the business.

Managing a company strategically embraces both thinking and action. It takes action on multiple fronts, moving seamlessly from one strategic issue to another, because it employs a multidimensional strategy. It calls for making hard choices, not false choices, such as that between growth and cost reduction. It derives strength from a both/and philosophy rather than an either/or dichotomy. Indeed, I would argue that, in a fundamental sense, the strength of strategy lies in its ability to harness the power of opposites—objectives, strategies, policies, or actions that may seem, on the surface, to be contradictory, even mutually exclusive, but have in reality to work together.

Take an elementary example. The first step in strategy development is, typically, a situation assessment (or SW/OTs analysis). This calls for us to identify both the opportunities and threats posed by the current and future environment and the strengths and weaknesses that the organization currently brings to the competitive fray. Strategy then calls for us to seize the opportunities, avert or minimize the threats, leverage our strengths, and correct our weaknesses—all at the same time (although the emphasis on each of these thrusts will not always be identical). It has to deal simultaneously with many strategic issues. In practice, strategy making and implementation is a highly complex task, taking its cues from the market, competitive, and sociopolitical environment and leading to the adoption of multiple courses of action. A business strategy is not a single cord, but a cable made up of the intertwining of multiple cords (a) marketing strategy, manufacturing strategy, technology strategy, organization strategy, public affairs strategy, and so on).

Almost from its inception, strategic planning has been distorted by a false dichotomy in both its theory and its practice. Theorists have divided into the intuitive (Mintzberg) and the analytical (Ansoff) schools, yet experience is clear that strategic planning will falter if it is not a blending of the two. Similarly, corporate and consulting practice has all too often tended to emphasize one objective or one methodology—reengineering, total quality management, share owner value, core competencies—to the neglect of others and the detriment of the whole. But history teaches us that lasting success depends on attaining multiple objectives.

THE VALUE OF BOTH/AND

In both theory and practice, both/and is a far more sound guiding principle than either/or. Admittedly, both as individuals and as managers, we seem to find it easier to make decisions based on simple either/or choices. However, in the complex world we live in, solutions cannot be this simple. Most frequently, the best, if not the only viable, solution forces us to embrace opposites. Consider, for example, the following pairs of opposites that turn out to be more complementary than conflicting.

Holding to a Strategic Vision versus Flexibility in Tactical Action

The tension between these seemingly polar ideas derives from the larger debate about the relative roles of luck and foresight in business success. Once again the answer is "Both!" It should be obvious that flexibility without vision is aimless, and vision without flexibility can be dangerous (as Cisco recently demonstrated—see Box 4.1).

In the next chapter I argue the case for developing a powerful and coherent vision, noting that a vision that is well communicated and well understood can increase, rather than decrease, an organization's ability to act flexibly in response to changes in the tactical situation. With a clear idea of where the organization is going and how it plans to get there, managers at every level are better able to determine what is the best course of action to take in the immediate situation. The vision provides the aim that will direct the fire.

However, this argument is not always well understood. For instance, when Lou Gerstner took over as chief executive officer of IBM, he made frequent statements to the effect that "the last thing IBM needs right now is a vision." Certainly, the case for immediate tactical action on cost reduction and improved market focus was obvious and inarguable. But

---

Box 4.1
Cisco: A Study in Denial

Cisco Systems is a case study of a company so committed to realizing its vision that it was unable to foresee, and act upon, the need for flexibility in its tactical responses to changes in a volatile environment.

The vision, as John Chambers, Cisco's CEO, put it, was to "change the world" through the widespread application of Internet technology to virtually every aspect of business while dominating the markets for the new infrastructure technology (e.g., networking gear, storage devices, optical equipment). Cisco's aim was to be the ultimate Internet company, networked with customers, employees, and suppliers, driven by an empowered work force, and growing dramatically through adroit marketing and a seemingly endless series of acquisitions. Everything that Cisco did seemed, for a while, to be faster, bigger, and better than any other company. Its stock traded at multiples in excess of 100; and, for one shining moment, it was the most valuable company in the world.

But the brightness of the vision blinded the company to the magnitude of the changes that were taking place in its markets during 2000–2001—a global economic recession, the collapse of telecoms demand, and the slaughter of aspiring dot.com companies. Cisco's vaunted information systems and links to customers and suppliers were supposed to keep the company tuned to the market but failed to override the preconceptions of executives who were committed to the vision and in denial regarding the extent of the changes going on around them.

As a result, instead of making flexible and timely adjustments, the company was forced into sudden and drastic actions, writing off $2.2 billion in excess inventory and laying off 8,500 employees. Since March 2000, Cisco's market valuation has been slashed by some $430 billion to $154 billion.

equally obvious was the need for an answer to the question, "After re-structuring, what?". Eventually, of course, Gerstner did develop his vision, "network-centric computing,"[1] and used it to unify and motivate a slimmed down, more agile and rejuvenated company (see Box 4.2).

Contrary to expectations, one of the essential characteristics of a viable vision is its flexibility. It must always be open and responsive to change. Flexibility does not mean abandoning the vision: it simply recognizes the need to tune the vision continually to the requirements of an ever-changing business environment.

Achieving Sales Growth versus Controlling Costs

This is perhaps one of the more topical of these supposed either/or dichotomies. How often do we read in the business press such statements as, "Managers are beginning to realize that repeated cost-cutting is no

---

Box 4.2
Blending Short-Term and Long-Term at IBM

Shortly after he was selected as IBM's CEO in 1993, Louis V. Gerstner was famously quoted as saying, "The last thing IBM needs right now is a vision." As a result, many branded him as yet another turnaround artist interested in nothing but short-term results, while others (including me) pointed out that IBM needed *both* short-term discipline and a new long-term vision. The next nine years were to show that Gerstner delivered on both scores. He made the tough short-term calls with massive layoffs, the sale of some operations, and the closing of several plants, offices, and projects. He introduced strict fiscal discipline, reenergized the culture, and heightened customer focus (for instance, by setting quotas for customer calls by senior executives). But he also came to recognize that IBM did, indeed, need a new vision to replace the then 20-year old hardware ("big iron") reputation that was fading rapidly.

His longer-term vision showed Gerstner's skills as a strategic thinker. Within two years, he saw the strategic significance of the Internet as a place to do business not just a place for consumer browsing, and this became the key to IBM's turnaround. Most importantly, Gerstner moved IBM away from its roots in hardware to a new emphasis on technology and services, thus positioning the company for today's trends in corporate IT, with companies wanting fewer products but a broader range of services and a way to make what they have work better.

The results speak for themselves. IBM is now in a more solid position than it has been for years, with $85.9 billion in revenues and $7.7 billion in profits in 2001. Perhaps even more significant is the fact that it has reshaped the industry: IBM is now the company whose strategy other companies seek to emulate.

longer the path to sustained profitable growth"? Set aside for the moment the implausibility that cost cutting could ever be considered a realistic path to *sustained* growth. If cost reduction or downsizing is an immediate strategic issue, management still has to determine which costs to reduce, which objectives downsizing should serve, and how to distinguish between organizational fat that must be trimmed and organizational muscle that the company must preserve, even strengthen, for future growth.

Implicit in this dichotomy is the notion that corporate strategy should oscillate between promoting growth in periods of economic expansion and rigorous cost controls in periods of economic contraction. There are at least two problems with such a notion. In the first place, these abrupt oscillations are the antithesis of a steady, coherent strategy: they are better characterized as responses to changes in the tactical situation. In the second place, both promoting growth without thought for its added costs and cutting costs without thought for its impact on growth are equally foolish and destructive responses to the situation.

However, we have examples of strategy that suggest such a dichotomy is counterproductive, that harnessing these two factors—growth and cost control—is the way to go. For example, in 1998 Renault sent Carlos Ghosn to Japan with instructions to turn around its ailing Japanese affiliate, Nissan. True to his nickname, "Le Cost Cutter," Ghosn began by slashing payroll costs and closing five factories. However, at the same time he was making these cuts, he was looking to increase sales by hiring designers from America with instructions to produce no fewer than 22 new models before the end of 2002.

Similarly, Stephen M. Wolff, the head of US Airways, foresaw the perils of such false choices. For several years, he confronted the twin imperatives of reducing the airline's costs (which are substantially above industry average) and promoting international expansion and alliances to expand the airline's service area. The strategy may not succeed, but this two-pronged approach is most surely the correct one.

However, while the future of US Airways's strategy may be up in the air (no pun intended!), there can be no denying the success of Jack Welch's multipronged strategy at GE. From the very start of his tenure as CEO in 1981, he clearly, and publicly, emphasized a both/and approach to strategy. On the one hand, he relentlessly slashed costs, reducing corporate staff and layers of management and attacking bureaucratic bloat wherever it was found. But, unlike Albert ("Chainsaw Al") Dunlap at Sunbeam, Welch gave equal emphasis to positioning the company for growth in services and high-technology markets and stressing the globalization initiative to increase the company's presence in faster growing overseas economies. As a result, while worldwide employment declined from 367,000 in 1982 (Welch's first year as CEO) to 223,000 in 2000, revenues increased from $26.5 billion to $129.8 billion. Clearly, a both/and approach to strategy succeeded brilliantly here.[2]

Perhaps the definitive statement on the fallacy of this supposed dichotomy is one made by Roger Enrico, when he was still vice chairman of Pepsico: "People who go through restructuring and downsizing without a plan for growth are the people who consume assets rather than invest in them."[3]

Meeting Market/Customer Needs versus Beating the Competition

It is almost inconceivable that this dichotomy should have attained the measure of respectability that it has. Yet if we listen carefully to executive pronouncements (particularly those in Annual Reports), two schools of thought clearly emerge. There are those who emphasize the Tom Peters' dictum of "getting close to your customer," arguing that understanding what your customers truly need and value is the essential basis for strategic success. And then there are those who take their cue from Michael Porter in emphasizing the critical importance of identifying and responding to the current and future sources of competition.

It is surely obvious that a market, by definition, is created by the interaction of two parties—buyer and seller and customers and competitive suppliers. In the words of the old song, you simply "can't have one without the other." It stand to reason, therefore, that any strategy must address both "opposites," both elements in this equation, at the same time. There are obvious dangers inherent in focusing on serving the customer without paying attention to what competitors are doing, or in single-mindedly striving to do what the competition does—only better. This simple and obvious fact tends, however, to get neglected in corporations' search for a single silver bullet. This is not so much the fault of gurus such as Peters and Porter as it is of their followers who seem to mistake the part (a) commendable focus on an admirable course of action) for the whole (the total strategy).

If we look for a model of a successful both/and approach in this domain, we need look no further than Michael Dell's model for his computer company. This model—built on direct dealings with customers, mass customization of manufacturing, the virtual elimination of inventory, and the inclusion of its suppliers in an electronic network—has catapulted Dell Computer Corporation to the number one position in the

PC market. Dell has succeeded both in giving customers what they want, when they want it, and in becoming the driving force in the industry, setting the model and the pace that his competitors must try to emulate.

Leading versus Following the Market

This pair of opposites reflects the old question in marketing strategy, "Is it better to be the market leader or a quick follower?" With all the talk these days about the strategic importance of "reinventing industries" and "changing the rules of the game," one might think that the answer had been given, clearly and definitively, in favor of market leadership. And the success of change leaders as varied as Dell Computer, Nike, Home Depot, and Starbucks Coffee would seem to put this answer beyond argument.

Yet the closer we look at such successes, the clearer it becomes that they are the result of *both* restructuring markets and industries *and* following the latent desires and needs of their customers, frequently developing product and services attributes that customers hadn't even thought of or didn't think were possible. In a fundamental sense, market leaders have, in effect, followed the dictates of the latent or potential market.

Lower Prices versus Higher Quality

In the old typology of competitive strategies, popularized by Michael Porter, you had to make a choice among quality, product differentiation, and cost as the basis on which you chose to compete. Quality came at a higher cost, it was argued, and quality products, therefore, had to be marketed to customers who were prepared to pay a higher price. With the coming of information technology, however, in many cases such a choice is no longer necessary: one can produce and market a higher quality product at a lower price. An obvious example of this phenomenon is offered by the microprocessor industry which has, over several generations of products, followed Moore's Law of doubling capacity and halving price every 18 months. Less well known is the case of Alaska Airlines, which, in the face of the entry of low-fare competitors into its markets, successfully executed a strategy that combined maintaining its top-notch service with slashing its fares.

We can also point to an increasing number of examples in the environmental arena, in which, until relatively recently, corporations have taken it as gospel that being "green" meant being uncompetitive in costs. No doubt that still can be the case when well-intentioned but badly exe-

cuted regulation tries to impose an inflexible solution on a complex problem. But, as Michael Porter and Amory Lovins have shown, it is
possible, by adopting a new approach to the problem, to be both green
and competitive.[4] As one example, 3M, when confronted with the need
to reduce solvent emissions by 90 percent, found a way to eliminate the
use of solvents altogether by using water-based solutions in their place.
In the process, the company shortened its time to market, reduced costs
(by eliminating the need for regulatory hearings), and gained a competitive advantage from developing a superior product.

The lesson here, at a minimum, is that we should hesitate to assume
that these opposites are totally incompatible—desired by customers, but
deemed impractical by producers.

Creative Destruction versus Exploitation of Existing Strengths

Fifty years ago, the economist Joseph Schumpeter coined the term
"creative destruction" to describe the process by which the competitive
enterprise system drives economic and social progress by constantly replacing existing products and systems with better and more efficient
ones, simultaneously destroying and creating. Today, the validity of
Schumpeter's theory is even more apparent in the rapid improvements
in products, process, and services brought about by technology and
competition.

In such an environment, a key element of corporate strategy must be
the application of "creative destruction" internally as well as externally,
spinning off lines of business or shutting them down to free the resources
for new ones, as Intel did when it decided to abandon the dynamic
random access memory (DRAM) business in favor of microprocessors.
Mere incremental change, like closing a facility, is not enough. Richard
Foster and Sarah Kaplan, in their book *Creative Destruction*, go so far
as to assert that corporations now have to behave like a private equity
firm, "trading out" and "trading in" quickly and ruthlessly.[5]

There is, however, a "Yes, but . . . " counterargument to their assertion.
Companies build up capabilities and competitive strengths over many
years, progressing down the learning curve. They thus have a major
investment in these assets and should not give them up without a great
deal of thought. Certainly, a single-minded (one might almost say "sim-
ple-minded") commitment to switching rather than fighting in the face
of every challenge would be a misbegotten strategy. Monsanto learned
a painful lesson in this regard when it sold its highly profitable Nutra-

sweet business to finance its ill-fated move into genetically modified agriculture. But even at best, when such a swap succeeds, there is an organizational price to pay for a constant shuffling of strategy and portfolio.

There is no easy answer, no single right answer, to the question: When should we switch? When should we fight back and innovate our way around a challenge?

E-business versus Traditional Business

At the height of the dot.com boom, amid widespread managerial uncertainty about the extent and significance of the so-called new economy, a clear-cut division of opinion existed between those who foresaw "clicks" replacing "bricks," the triumph of a new business model over the old, and those who felt that E-business would turn out to be much ado about very little. Now, in the wake of the dot.com collapse, the both/ and implications of the Internet are becoming clearer. As Michael Porter noted, in a *Business Week* interview, "We need to see the Internet as complementary to other things the company does rather than contradictory or cannibalistic."[6]

It is not a matter of one business model replacing another. Nor is it primarily a matter of specific technologies such as the advent of the personal computer, the proliferation of E-mail, or the popularity of the Internet. Rather it is a matter of using a new strategic tool to enhance a firm's unique strategy. As Porter said in the same interview, "If you view it as a strategic tool, you'll ask yourself: 'O.K., given my product concept and how I try to differentiate myself, how can I use the Internet to make that differentiation stronger?'"

Jack Welch saw that clearly enough when, in 1999, he told GE managers that E-business would be every division's "priority one, two, three, and four," and announced "Destroyyourbusiness.com"—a mandate to each division to reinvent itself before someone else did. The aim was, as he said in GE's annual report, to use E-business to "change the DNA of GE forever by energizing and revitalizing every corner of this company."

Social/Political Factors versus Economic Realities

In the traditional management view, social responsibility was defined as community relations, charitable donations, and aid to education—nice things to do, if you could afford them, but definitely peripheral to the main thrusts of strategy, which were to deal with the hard facts of market and competitive realities.

Now, however. with a changing social, economic, and political climate, social responsibility (or, more accurately, "social and political responsiveness") has been redefined in terms that are central to corporate strategy. In my book, *The New Rules of Corporate Conduct,* I identified seven key thrusts of a social strategy for corporations as the issues of corporate legitimacy, governance, environmental strategy, the new employment contract, public-private sector relationships, equity, and ethics.[7]

Whatever position a corporation might take on these issues, it must deal with them at the same level of importance and executive attention as the pressing needs to respond to radical shifts in markets, competition, and technology. Doing good and doing well are more closely linked than ever before in an era when public interest groups are multiplying and class action suits routinely seek damages for hundreds of millions of dollars. Both corporate strategy and executive leadership now need to deal, equally and simultaneously, with both sociopolitical and competitive measures of corporate performance, once conceived as opposites and contradictory, but now as parallel and intertwined requirements for corporate success.

The need for a both/and approach to this problem is evident in the case of two well-known reformer companies—the health and beauty retailer The Body Shop, and ice-cream makers Ben & Jerry. The Body Shop founder, Anita Roddick, favored natural ingredients, opposed testing cosmetics on animals, and promoted ethical trading with African farmers and the peoples of Latin American rain forests. Ben Cohen and Jerry Greenfield gave 7.5 percent of pretax profits to charities and 5 percent to employees and espoused causes such as voter registration and opposition to the Gulf War. These campaigns, reinforced by quality products, translated into substantial marketing advantage but were not sufficient to ensure the companies' success in tough competitive times. Ben & Jerry's was sold to Unilever, and Anita and Gordon Roddick were forced out of their management roles in The Body Shop. The problem in each case rested not with the cost of these social initiatives but with the inability of the companies to deal with the basic economic needs of the business. Neither company was particularly well run: The Body Shop was unable to manage its expansion into global markets, and Ben & Jerry's suffered from poor employee morale (despite the profit sharing) and even failed to keep up with McDonald's in using chlorine-free packaging materials.

For more corporate evidence, consider the case of Douglas Ivester,

CEO of Coca-Cola Company. Described by the *Wall Street Journal* as a brilliant and driven financial strategist, the Coke board saw him as the logical successor to Roberto Guizeta as chairman and CEO. Yet almost from the outset of his tenure, it became apparent that he lacked the ability to manage social strategy, having what the *Journal* termed a "tin ear" for public and political nuances. His clumsy handling of one public relations and political flap after another costs him the board's confidence and led him to announce his intention to step down and make way for fresh leadership. Significantly, the board then selected Douglas Daft, an executive with a stronger record of dealing with both the competitive and sociopolitical aspects of strategy.

Even the inimitable Jack Welch stumbled in this arena by underestimating the strength of European political opposition to the proposed GE-Honeywell merger. Having received signals of prospective approval for the deal from U.S. antitrust authorities, Welch thought that gaining the approval of the European Commission would be relatively straightforward. What he failed to understand, or underestimated, was the fact that the United States and European Commission used essentially different criteria in assessing such mergers. In the United States, the primary consideration is the potential impact on customers; in the European Commission , it is the impact on competitors. This was one occasion when Welch failed to heed his own advice on the need to understand "where you sit in today's world. *Not where you wish you were and where you hoped you would be, but where you are*" (emphasis added—see the full quote in Chapter 3).[8]

Long Term versus Short Term

Perhaps the best known pair of opposites is the classic debate between long-term and short-term perspectives in management. Assuredly, one aim of a corporation is to look beyond the immediate present in an effort to perpetuate itself: but to do that, it must, of course, deal successfully with the current situation. So the need for a duality of perspectives should be obvious.

Analysts often compare U.S. managers unfavorably with Japanese managers because of their emphasis on short-term profits and relative lack of long-term perspective. Too often, U.S. managers' response to such criticism is either that the Japanese are particularly blessed (by lower interest rates and so-called patient capital of *keiretsu* holdings), or that U.S. CEOs cannot buck either the market or the security analysts whose only interests, it is said, are in the next quarter. Such a response first accepts the validity of the charge and then attempts to explain the reason for this situation.

However, this argument, as *Fortune* pointed out many years ago, "widely accepted as gospel, poses just one problem: it isn't valid."[9] The article went on to quote research showing that investors do, in fact, place considerable value on profits that won't materialize for 5 to 10 years, and that the market does not necessarily hammer a stock that reports disappointing quarterly results, if investors (particularly institutional investors) perceive the dip as a one-time quirk which management has taken steps to reverse. Alfred Rappaport, professor of accounting and finance at Northwestern University's Kellogg School and a leading student of stock values, developed a model of how the market sets stock prices based on such key value drivers as expected sales growth, operating profit margins, investments to sustain growth, and the cost of capital. According to Rappaport, speaking from a late-1980s perspective, "You can't justify today's stock prices without looking at profits into the 21st. century."

Quite apart from the stock market's evaluation, however, the strategic record of the past 20 years demonstrates the need for companies to attend to long-term and short-term issues simultaneously. Business history is replete with examples of companies such as General Motors, AT&T, and Xerox in the United States, Olivetti in Italy, Hitachi in Japan, and Philips in the Netherlands that were once brilliantly successful in producing short-term results but failed to consider long-term changes in their markets and competition. The opposite can also be true. In the early 1990s, CEO Richard Ferris' vision for Allegis Corporation (as he renamed United Airlines) as a full-service travel company, including hotels and car rentals, was conceptually sound, but it collapsed in part because of his failure to deal with the immediate problems of poor financial performance.

More recently, many dot.com ventures have had the right long-term vision but have stumbled in their handling of short-term problems in production costs and consumer marketing. Gary Hamel, arguing in *Fortune* for the reality of first-mover advantage, noted that "most pioneering dot-coms failed, not because they were first, but because they were dumb," for instance, by getting their timing wrong, overpaying for market share, or "being first with a business model that's DOA."[10]

In its 2001 Annual Report, Intel Corporation put these short- and long-term perspectives in a historical context, looking at the course of two technologies—steel and rail—over the past two centuries. History has shown that major technological revolutions have ridden waves of boom and bust, only to rebound with periods of sustained growth. Steel and rail technologies evolved through birth, turbulence, and build-out:

- *Birth.* Enabling technologies emerge, innovations flourish, pioneers crowd the field, early investors make extraordinary profits, fueling speculation and irrational exuberance.
- *Turbulence.* Overinvestment and overcapacity burst the bubble, stock prices drop, some companies fold, and investment halts.
- *Build-out.* Confidence returns, and real value emerges. Missing components of the technology are developed, and the technology penetrates the economy. Sustained investment yields robust returns, and the technology becomes the driving engine of the economy.

Intel sees the Internet revolution following this historical pattern of rail and steel, with its most rewarding years yet to come. Despite short-term pressures, therefore, the company maintained its long-term strategy, including what might seem to be a counterintuitive acceleration of capital investment, spending $7.3 billion in 2001 compared with $10 billion in capital spending over the previous two years combined.

For more successful examples of this blending of short- and long-term perspectives, we can look to IBM and Nokia. The IBM example is described in Box 4.2. As for Nokia, under its dynamic CEO, Jorma Ollila, it has evolved a winning formula that combines foresight in reading the nature, direction, and timing of market changes with excellence in execution, quality in products and processes, and speed in fulfilling customer needs. "When something has been achieved, developments are already somewhere else," Ollila has observed. "I'm always looking at the next challenge."[11] What is remarkable about these two examples is the fact that they occurred in adverse conditions—Gerstner's turnaround of a crippled IBM, and Ollila's effort to build a little known Finnish company into a global powerhouse. Against the odds, both succeeded.

Welch, as usual, is gutsy and straight to the point on this paradox. "Any fool could do one or the other," he has noted, by squeezing out costs at the expense of the future, or dreaming about the future but failing to deliver in the short term. "The test of a leader is balancing the two."[12]

SO WHAT SHOULD WE DO?

Confronted with such an overwhelming array of apparently contradictory advice, most executives would tend to shy away from any attempt to deal with such a challenge, opting instead for a simpler, albeit less comprehensive, approach. Even if we recognize that some of the contradictions are more apparent than real, and that the "opposites" are, in truth, not contradictory but complementary—even then the challenge is daunting. And it is made even more intimidating by the fact that it is not feasible to give any straightforward guidance on how to deal with this challenge. It is not a simple matter of *balancing* each pair, for such a term suggests, erroneously, that we should give equal emphasis to each factor, when in reality the relative emphasis on each factor must vary with the situation in which each company finds itself.

Perhaps the best advice one can give an executive confronted with this dilemma is, "For every strategic thrust that you plan, consider also how you will deal with its reciprocal." History is replete with examples of companies that went for broke by betting on a good idea—and ended up broke because they failed to consider its reciprocal. There is no formula, no algorithm, we can use as an easy fix for this dilemma.

There is, however, an approach to the problem that I have found helpful: profiling the strategy. As shown in Box 4.3, it is possible to develop a profile—first, of the current strategy, and then, of the desired strategy—in terms of their treatment of each pair of opposites. Such an approach is, of course, entirely a matter of judgment and is only a graphic representation of reality: and it will not, by itself, give any easy answers. It will, however, provide a useful frame of reference for a strategic dialogue.

It is not only in strategy that the creative power of opposites comes into play. In a fascinating article in *Fortune,* Gary Hamel noted that, in these turbulent times, business leaders should turn to history to learn how America's resilience has stemmed in large part from a series of tensions that the country "holds in perpetual creative balance."[13] What are these tensions? Hamel cites five in particular:

- Value coherence, celebrate diversity
- Love the community, honor the activist
- Be strong, show compassion
- Be courageous, practice prudence
- Revere the timeless, embrace the new.

The lesson of history would seem to be that, in any large venture, there are seldom any simple guidelines. Walt Whitman said it best in "Song of Myself": "Do I contradict myself? Very well then, I contradict myself. I am large, I contain multitudes."

Box 4.3
"Profiling" the Opposites

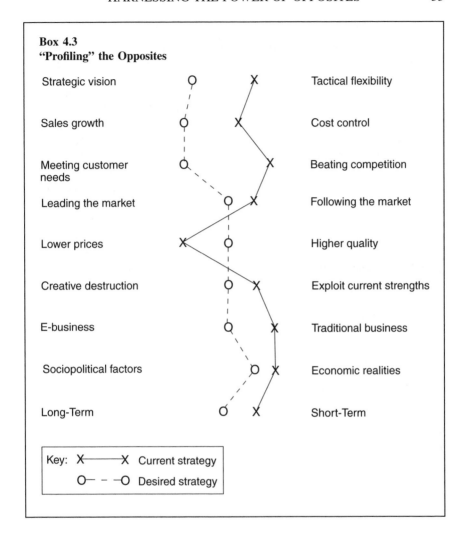

Strategic vision		Tactical flexibility
Sales growth		Cost control
Meeting customer needs		Beating competition
Leading the market		Following the market
Lower prices		Higher quality
Creative destruction		Exploit current strengths
E-business		Traditional business
Sociopolitical factors		Economic realities
Long-Term		Short-Term

Key: X———X   Current strategy
O– – –O   Desired strategy

NOTES

1. "The View from IBM: Lou Gerstner Does Have a Vision," *Business Week,* 30 October 1995.

2. For a fuller account of Welch's strategy, see the section on "Vision at Work in General Electric" in chapter 4.

3. Quoted in *Fortune,* 7 March 1994.

4. See, for example, two articles appearing in the *Harvard Business Review*—Michael E. Porter and Claas van der Linde, "Green **and** Competitive," September–October 1995; and Amory B. Lovins, L. Hunter Lovins, and Paul Hawken, "A Road Map for Natural Capitalism" (May–June 1999).

5. Richard Foster and Sarah Kaplan, *Creative Destruction: Why Companies*

That Are Built to Last Underperform the Market—And How to Successfully Transform Them (New York: Doubleday, 2001).

6. Michael E. Porter, "Caught in the Net," interview, *Business Week,* 27 August 2001.

7. Ian Wilson, *The New Rules of Corporate Conduct: Rewriting the Social Charter* (Westport, Conn.: Quorum Books, 2000) (See also Box 8.1).

8. See the fascinating and detailed account of Welch's encounters with Commissioner Mario Monti on this deal, in the chapter entitled "Go Home, Mr. Welch," in his autobiography, *Jack: Straight from the Gut.*

9. "Yes, You Can Manage Long Term," *Fortune,* 21 November 1988.

10. Gary Hamel, "Smart Mover, Dumb Mover," *Fortune,* 3 September 2001.

11. Dan Steinbock, *The Nokia Revolution* (New York: American Management Association, 2001).

12. JackWelch, with John A. Byrne, *Jack: Straight from the Gut* (New York: Warner Business Books, 2001), 124.

13. Gary Hamel, "What CEOs Can Learn from America," *Fortune,* 12 November 2001.

Chapter 5

THE POWER OF STRATEGIC VISION

It was the second day of a two-day strategy workshop that I was leading. The day was hot, and after two full days of demanding exercises evaluating strategic options for the company the participants' intellectual and energy levels were low. The CEO leaned back in his chair, fixed me with a hard stare, and asked, with doubt and a tinge of sarcasm coloring his voice, "Do we really have to go though all this vision stuff? "Why can't we go to the Board," he asked, with exasperation and genuine perplexity, "with what we've already done?"

"Because what we have," I said, "doesn't yet hang together. Because it doesn't have the power to reshape the company and energize its strategy. Because it lacks the driving force that will command the commitment of your managers and employees. Because what we have will be difficult to sell to the financial community." My response was, admittedly, impromptu and emotional. Given more time and a cooler day, I might have marshaled my arguments more calmly.

This episode, more than any other single experience, crystallized in my mind the conviction that corporations are, typically, overmanaged and underled. For nothing sets the leader apart from the manager than a belief in—and the use of—the power of strategic vision. And my own appreciation of this power has led me on a long crusade to define vision more precisely; to lay out a process for its development; and to persuade others to incorporate its power into their strategic thinking and action.

COMING TO GRIPS WITH VISION

Vision is the central driving force of strategic management, so it is worth spending some time discussing its nature, uses, and power. To begin with, it is clearly differentiated from the first definition in *The New Webster Encyclopedic Dictionary of the English Languate* (1980 edition): "something seen in a dream, trance, or the like."[1] Yet this is the popular perception of the term: most executives equate *visionary* with *impractical* and consider discussion of this idea unbusinesslike at best and a foolish waste of time and distraction from the important business of strategy at worst. Even those who admit the need for leadership and acknowledge the role of vision tend to believe that vision is largely a soft and indefinable term and that existing examples are idiosyncratic.

I have in mind something that is harder, more substantive, and easier to replicate in a wide variety of organizations. Webster's has another definition that comes closer to what I have in mind: vision, the dictionary says, is "the ability to perceive something not actually visible, as through mental acuteness and keen foresight."[2] That definition does capture some of the qualities that I have in mind when I use the term, but it does not go far enough. In corporate terms,[3] I define strategic vision as, "A coherent and powerful statement of what the business can, and should, be (10) years hence" (the time horizon varies, of course, with the nature of the business). I have deliberately kept the definition succinct, simple and (I) hope) jargon free. But each term in this definition is carefully chosen and important.

The vision must be *coherent*—that is, it should pull together mission, goals, strategies, and action plans into a complete and recognizable picture of the future company and how it got there. It is the product of the holistic thinking that is one of the essential qualities of strategy. In effect, the vision says, "If our assessment of the future is correct, and we succeed in doing everything that our strategy has planned, this is what the company would look like."

Second, the vision must be *powerful*—that is, it should be capable of generating strong commitment and motivating superior performance. To do this, the vision needs to be inspiring, and to be inspiring, it needs to set goals that are demanding and are perceived by employees and other stakeholders to be worthy of their efforts. That is one reason why the best visions reach beyond purely financial goals to set a program of action that becomes, in effect, a crusade.

Third, the vision emphasizes what the business *can* be because it must be realistic in its assessment of what is attainable in the market, the competitive, economic, and regulatory environment in which the company operates, and what the company's real capabilities are. One of the grave dangers in shaping a vision is to allow it to become unrealistic in an effort to be challenging. Certainly, a vision needs to set stretch goals that demand much of everyone in the organization, but the goals themselves must be realistic. For instance, it was quite realistic for Jack Welch to set a goal for GE of being, or becoming, number one or number two in each of the business areas in which it operated, but it was quite inappropriate for many other companies that mimicked Welch's goals and set similar targets which were, for them, quite unrealistic.

And, finally, the vision should clarify what the business *should* be because it should reflect the values and aspirations of management, employees, and other stakeholders. In sum, the vision is part rational, that is, it is the product of analysis, and part emotional, the product of imagination, hunches, and values. We might say that vision embodies both the yang and the yin of corporate strategy and performance.

Vision, thus defined, embraces, but goes beyond, strategic concept and driving force—ideas such as Jan Carlzon's characterization of Scandinavian Airlines System (SAS)) in the 1980s as "the businessman's airline," or Koji Kobayashi's emphasis on "C&C" (the link between computer and communications) as the key element in his vision for NEC, the Japanese electronics conglomerate. Such ideas are, of course, central to strategy, but (for me) lack the completeness of a fully developed strategic vision.

In an effort to convey the breadth and significance of my definition, I once described strategic vision to an Australian planner as "a preview of the annual report 10 years hence." Six months later, he sent me his draft of what might be his managing director's report to shareholders in that future year, detailing not only the mix of businesses and their financial results, but also the company's diversification moves, organizational restructuring, and the state of union relations—all in the context of reviewing the intervening years of change in the economy and their industry.

Although one need not take my future-annual-report analogy quite as literally as my Australian friend did, I do urge CEOs and companies to move toward that level of detail in their visioning. I strongly believe that, if a vision is to inspire and motivate, it should convey to the listener or reader a good feel for the size, shape, style, and texture of the future company, and how it got that way.

THE CASE FOR VISION

Given the urgency of present problems and the uncertainty of future ones, it is not surprising that busy executives might wonder—as the CEO did in my opening example—why they should bother to engage in what many of them perceive to be an academic exercise. Visioning, after all, takes time; it supplements, rather than supplants, traditional strategic planning, and it is seen, at best, as an uncertain exercise, with questionable benefits.

But I would argue that vision is needed precisely for the same reasons strategic planning is—namely, that we live in uncertain times. In a more stable, predictable era, a momentum strategy and incremental changes may be acceptable—not inspiring, but workable. It is the very uncertainty and volatility of the current business environment that makes for discontinuity in corporate direction and demands radical—and rapid—rather than incremental change in strategies, direction, and action.

Some will argue, I know, that the degree of uncertainty and discontinuity is such that the best we can do is to be flexible and ready to respond rapidly to the unexpected. But, critical though it may be as an organizational (and personal) characteristic, flexibility is not a strategy. It establishes no goals and sets no direction. And, as the saying goes, "If you don't know where you're going, it doesn't matter how you get there."

Vision, on the other hand, clearly establishes both a direction and a destination. It is the star we can steer by as we sail the turbulent and uncharted waters of the future.

Vision is needed, too, as the capstone and integrating mechanism for the elements of strategic planning—mission and philosophy, goals and objectives, strategy and action plans, and organization structure and culture (see Figure 3.1: The Flow of Strategic Management). It sums up all these elements into a complete picture of the future company and helps to strengthen the coherence and internal consistency of its component parts. With a strategic vision in place, we can see the *total* picture and ask: Does that truly represent what we want to become? Is it complete? Realistic? Achievable? Do strategy, organization, and culture fit together? It forces us to see the future business as a piece, rather than as piecemeal.

Finally, vision is needed as a force for empowering and implementation. Make no mistake: it is not my contention that vision *alone* accomplishes anything. Experience has taught us that the execution of strategy is a complex and, at times, frustrating problem for which no single solution is possible. However, vision is linked to the dynamic power of leadership and, as I shall argue later, plays a key role in implementation. Hopefully, too, the vision is also, in some sense, inspiring and can generate enthusiasm and commitment for the tasks ahead.[4]

VISION AT WORK AT GE

There is no better example of the potential synergy between vision and operating management than the experience at GE over the past 20 years. From the first day that Jack Welch took over as CEO from Reginald H. ("Reg") Jones, he articulated, strongly, clearly, and consistently, a powerful vision that helped transform the company and, at the same time, deliver stellar financial results.[5] Welch's vision focused on two key elements: a restructuring of the business portfolio and a revitalization of the culture. He consistently implemented these two elements in tandem, although, for the first six or seven years, portfolio restructuring was the first priority; it was not until about 1988 that the culture change became the prime concern.

His vision of a restructured portfolio embraced a central image and a basic concept. The central image was one of three interlocking circles: one represented the remaining GE core or heritage businesses (for instance, lighting, turbines, and major appliances); another, the high-technology businesses (such as medical systems, plastics, and aircraft engines); and the third, high-growth services (such as financial and information services, and the National Broadcasting Corporation). Welch sought to discourage the notion that GE was a traditional conglomerate by emphasizing the integrated diversity of the three circles, with the core businesses benefiting from a transfer of technology and services offerings, high tech needing a link to services, and services relying on the latest technology to be competitive. An important point in this vision was the fact that it cut some businesses *out,* as well as cutting others in; notable among those excluded were the highly profitable resource businesses of Utah International and the more marginal small appliances.

The basic concept in this portfolio strategy was that GE would be only in those businesses in which it was (or could become) number one or number two in the global market (or, in the case of services, have a substantial position) and that were of a scale and potential appropriate to a company of GE's size.

From the outset, however, Welch saw the need for GE to become a different *type* of company—not just in its portfolio of businesses, but also in its culture, management values, and operating behavior—if it was to remain competitive in its markets. This was an evolving part of the vision, starting out with an emphasis on reducing the layers of management (from nine to as few as four levels) and moving to become what Welch famously termed a "boundaryless company"—that is, one in which the bureaucratic boundaries among functions, layers of management, and business units would become less restrictive and cooperation and sharing of ideas would become a way of life to the greater good of both the parts (individual business units) and the whole (the company as an integrated entity).

Welch's aim in revitalizing the corporate culture was to combine (as he put it) the sensitivity, the leanness, the simplicity, and the agility of a small company with the strength, resources, and reach of a big company. This could be achieved, he saw, only by pushing authority and responsibility down throughout the organization, empowering (as the new buzzword had it) managers by encouraging a more entrepreneurial spirit, drastically reducing the numbers and power of corporate staff, and then empowering employees, by means of the notable Work-Out process that sought to capture the ideas, the imagination, and the commitment of the entire work force.

Looking over the 20-year history of this vision, one cannot help being impressed by the central role that it played in Welch's leadership and by the ways in which he periodically redefined and reenergized it while adhering to its central and unchanging principles. In his major decisions, in his everyday actions, and in his communications inside and outside the company, Welch persistently and eloquently come back to the basic precepts of this vision: they have given force, guidance, and motivation to his actions and those of managers and employees at every level. When he was criticized for his pact with the French electronics firm, Thomson, which exchanged GE's consumer electronics business for their medical diagnostics unit, he could point to the portfolio image of the three circles—with consumer electronics (and, at the time, other businesses) lying outside them—as the logic for his decision. When he introduced the Work-Out program as a grassroots effort to tap the ideas and energy of every employee, people could see that it was not a feel-good or public relations ploy but a central part of his strategy to transform the working climate of the company.

Periodically, too, he reenergized the vision by focusing on new, companywide initiatives that are changing the way the company conducts its business. First came the globalization initiative, progressively moving the company from exports, to local production, to global sourcing, and finally to drawing on intellectual capital from all over the world. Next came the product services initiative based on the recognition that GE should not try to compete in the low-end, so-called wrench-turning game, but rather move into the high-technology, customer-productivity business, using tomorrow's technology to upgrade yesterday's hardware. Third was the Six Sigma quality initiative that progressed from projects to improve efficiency and product quality to its current emphasis on "helping customers win." Most recently came the E-business initiative with Welch's injunction to his managers—"Destroyyourbusiness.com"— rethink and remake your business before someone else does.

THE ELEMENTS OF VISION

A careful parsing of Welch's vision for GE shows that it is carefully crafted from at least six elements that fit together to form a harmonious whole:

- It describes the future focus of the company, the portfolio of businesses toward which GE would evolve.
- It establishes a critical goal, and defines a key criterion for success: each business should aim to be number one or two in its market (a) goal that Siemens of Germany, Electrolux of Sweden, and other companies have since adopted).
- The vision emphasizes the strategic importance of technology and service as the prime sources of competitive advantage in every business, not just in high-tech or service-oriented businesses.
- Welch sought to discourage the notion of conglomerateness by emphasizing integrated diversity, and demonstrating the interdependence of the three business arenas that were to form the future focus of the company.
- The vision defines the management roles and structure of the company, envisioning a flatter organization in which all the strategic business units reported directly to Welch and his vice chairmen.
- Finally, the vision portrays a revitalized culture, a lean and agile organization, and a boundaryless company.

Particularly significant is the fact that Welch's vision discussed not only content (the business concept) but also form (management structure and organization) and style (corporate culture).

A look at another impressive example—Jan Carlzon's vision for SAS when he was CEO—reveals a similar pattern:

- *Business concept.* SAS will be the "businessman's airline," integrating travel services for the busy executive.

- *Organization.* The company will rely heavily on joint ventures to build a global network of routes (a) particularly important strategy for an airline that started as just a regional player).
- *Culture.* The corporate culture will empower employees at every level to respond to customers' needs and problems. In his book, *Moments of Truth,* Carlzon spells out this part of his vision, noting that an airline's image and reputation are the product of thousands of "moments of truth" each day when travelers encounter SAS employees.

In my model (Figure 5.1) I emphasize six elements in an effort to ensure the completeness and coherence of vision: scope, scale, market focus, competitive focus, image and relationships, and organization and culture.

Business Scope

Business scope, the range and mix of businesses that the company chooses to pursue, is clearly a starting point for the vision. This calls for

Figure 5.1
The Elements of Strategic Vision

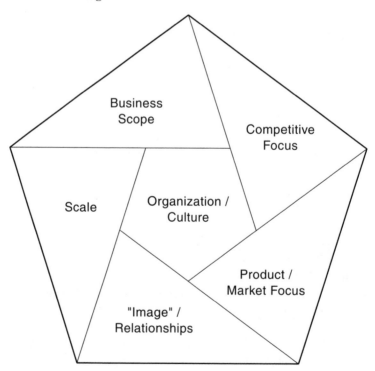

far more than just cataloging lines of business. It should sharpen the strategic focus of the company and identify target areas for both diversification and divestiture. It also calls for some tough strategic decisions, as it did for Jack Welch when he chose to divest GE of the resource businesses of Utah International, not because they were unprofitable (on the contrary, Utah accounted for a disproportionately large share of GE's total earnings), but simply because they did not fit into his strategic vision. That is the key: this element of vision should cut some things out, as well as cutting other things in. It is, in the best sense of the word, discriminating. Several years ago, in a strategic reevaluation of its direction, the former Foremost-McKesson Company chose to focus on value-added services to druggists, even though this required divesting its heritage dairy business and changing the corporate name to McKesson Corporation. Now, with the onset of global competition and the consequent need to be world class in everything that the corporation does, this need for sharpness and clarity in corporate focus has been redoubled.

Business Scale

Business scale, the desired future size of the company, must be another key element of the vision. When I was working with the management team of a Canadian chemical company, one of the senior vice presidents challenged me on this point, arguing that growth per se is not necessarily a sound objective. I countered that while that may be true, growth is normally an indicator of vitality, and a vision without scale would be incomplete. Scale—how large the company might be 5 or 10 years down the road—is a critical dimension of vision, if for no other reason than its impact on key elements of strategy. The difference between, say, doubling in size and remaining at roughly the same scale significantly affects marketing strategy, portfolio selection, investment needs, organization structure, management systems, and so on.

Product and Market Focus

Product and market focus represents a further sharpening of scope (the strategic focus of the corporation) through the identification of specific product lines and market niches that the company chooses to pursue. The pharmaceutical company that decides, for instance, to limit its scope to ethical prescription drugs must go one step further and chose which therapeutic categories (cancer, anti-infective, cardiovascular, etc.) and which segments of the medical community (doctors, hospital chains, health maintenance organizations, nursing homes, etc.) it will serve.

Competitive Focus

Probably nothing determines the future character of a company than its answer to the question: On what basis do we intend to compete? Will the company derive its competitive edge from technology (as GE does), direct dealings with customers (as Dell Computer does), convenience (as 7-Eleven does), or service (as SAS does)? Whatever the answer, it must go beyond mere words to influence every action and every decision, and become—in the term used by Benjamin Tregoe and John Zimmerman, in their book *Top Management Strategy*—the "driving force" of the company.[6]

Image and Relationships

Here the overlap between vision and statements of corporate values is perhaps greatest. However, the goal here should be to transcend philosophical generalities and specify the vital organizational dynamics necessary to implement the vision. Take, for instance, Jan Carlzon's insistence on empowering employees to make critical operating decisions to deal with customer problems. This was not merely a matter of good employee relations: it was a prerequisite for implementing the service strategy needed for SAS to become the successful "businessman's airline."

Organization and Culture

It is hard to imagine a complete vision statement without some insight into the future structure and operating climate of the company. Both structure and culture are integral elements of vision because both are essential to its successful implementation. Campbell Soup, for example, restructured its organization on a regional basis to match the regional thrust of its marketing strategy. And GE's emphasis on a revitalized culture as a central element in Jack Welch's vision has triggered similar action by many imitators.

SHAPING THE VISION

Developing a strategic vision does not do away with normally accepted planning steps. Nor is it a panacea or a stand-alone methodology. It is, rather, an integral part of strategic management[7] and adds value to this process by integrating the products of strategic planning into a coherent and meaningful whole.

The main danger in attempting to describe a process (useful though this may be) for developing a strategic vision is that it inevitably appears to emphasize rational analysis and sequential thinking and to ignore or downplay the roles of intuition and inspiration. Yet most of us would say that a truly visionary statement has a large element of such soft thinking. Indeed, both qualities are necessary. The need for a rational process of thought, formal or informal, goes hand in hand with the need for imagination.

Inevitably, at some point in my emphasis on the power of vision, I will be confronted with the question: "Yes, but how do you go about developing a vision?" (And, if the questioner is particularly doubting, the added question/comment, "Do you go into some sort of trance?!"). What follows is the essence of my reply to such a question, more in the form of loose guidelines than as set procedure.

1. *The visioning process is typically an iterative one.* The sometimes hazy outlines of a vision may emerge from, or even precede, the early analysis of the future business environment. This largely conceptual image can then inspire the exploration of new strategic options. It takes on greater substance and detail as executives establish strategic objectives, goals, and strategies. Finally, it becomes the capstone of strategic thinking, embodying the organization's goals and aspirations, and serving as the central driver of action. A vision gains clarity and strength from tentative formulation, reflection and analysis, testing, revisiting, and revising. Far better, therefore, to introduce it earlier in the project and work on it in tandem with other strategic analyses, allowing time for it to evolve toward completion.

2. *The process can be outlined as a series of eight key steps,* which are illustrated in Figure 5.2 and described in greater detail in Box 5.1:

   • Analyze the company's future environment (to arrive at an answer to the question: "What will the future allow or force us to be?")

   • Analyze the company's resources and capabilities ("Realistically, what can we be?")

   • Clarify management values ("What do we want to be?")

   • Develop (or revise) a mission statement

   • Identify strategic objectives and goals

   • Generate and select strategic options

   • Develop the vision statement

   • Conduct sanity checks

Figure 5.2
Developing a Strategic Vision

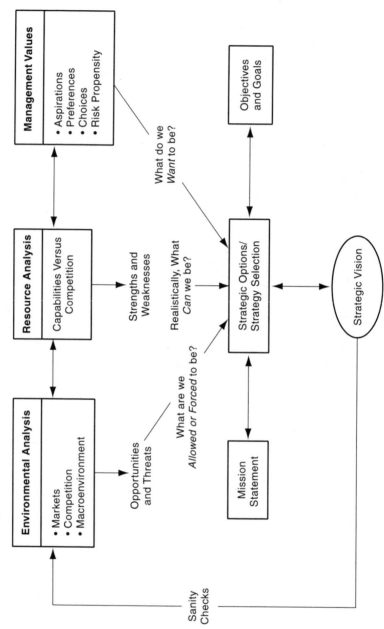

Box 5.1
An Eight-Step Visioning Process

If a collective visioning process is used, it is clearly necessary to inject somewhat more structure into the process than if it is an individual visioning exercise. However, the process must not be so restrictive that it curtails creativity and improvisation. In broad terms, the process I have followed when working with executive teams involves a series of workshops (typically, over a three- to four-month period), and incorporates eight key steps that, as will be seen, closely follow familiar stages of strategic thinking.

1. *Analyze the company's future business environment.* A detailed examination of likely scenarios of future market and competitive conditions, trends in the macroenvironment, and stakeholders' expectations can identify opportunities and threats likely to confront the company. Even the largest and most powerful of corporations cannot escape the impact of these trends, as Jack Welch found out belatedly ("You're never too old to be surprised") when the European regulators vetoed the proposed GE-Honeywell merger. In effect, this analysis seeks to answer the question, "What will the future allow or force us to be?"

2. *Analyze the company's resources and capabilities.* It is critically important to assess as objectively as possible the company's actual or potential competitive strengths and weaknesses in responding to such futures. Only when a company measures itself against the harsh external requirements of competition to meet changing customer needs can a true assessment of strengths and weaknesses emerge. This analysis, thus, seeks to answer the question, "Realistically, what can we become?"

3. *Clarify management values.* Too often, managers fail to articulate their values, or do so imperfectly, assuming that everyone on the organization shares a set of common values—such as risk propensity, desired rate of growth, and management style—when often they do not. Clarifying what the actual values are seeks to answer the question, "What do we want to be?" This question makes the important assumption that managers must always make choices in this exercise and that clarifying values helps make these choices (and the rationale for them) explicit.

4. *Develop (or revise) a mission statement.* A mission statement should define, in broad terms, the business arenas and purposes that the company will serve. Often, a mission statement is already in existence, but it should be revisited, and probably revised, in light of the findings from the previous steps. Writing this statement should be a creative exercise, broadly and imaginatively defining the markets or customer needs that the company will serve rather than the products and services it will offer. Thus, VISA has defined its business, not as issuing credit cards, but rather as "enabling customers to exchange value for virtually anything, anywhere in the world"—a much broader, and imaginative, mission.

5. *Identify strategic objectives and goals.* In effect, identifying strategic objectives is to define the future agenda of the company. Objectives specify the company's broad aims in pursuit of its mission, such as, "Achieve a better balance between domestic and offshore business," or "Develop a preeminent position in customer service." Goals, on the other hand, mark the milestones along the road to achieving these objectives: "Offshore sales account for 30 percent of total sales by 2003," or "Attain, by 2005, and maintain the number one position in industry surveys of customer satisfaction with service."

6. *Generate and select strategic options.* Strategy is—as I keep on saying—a matter of choice: certainly, a visionary strategy must be so. Therefore, managers need to stretch their imaginations to devise alternate strategies—different, creative ways of dealing with future opportunities and threats and strengths and weaknesses. Using scenarios in the first step is certainly helpful in opening up executives' minds to different possible futures and so to the need for different strategies to meet differing conditions. The final choice, therefore, is based on a careful assessment of the pros and cons of each option.

7. *Develop the vision statement.* As I have already pointed out, the vision usually emerges in stages rather than springing full-blown from the executive mind (individual or collective) at one point in time. What is intended here is the description of the final product. A simple, though mechanistic, approach is to progress through the six key elements of the vision—scope, scale, product and market focus, competitive focus, image and relationships, and organization and culture—as they are desired to be 5 or 10 years hence, completing each in turn, and then harmonizing the whole.

8. *Conduct sanity checks.* A final sanity check is absolutely critical. To ensure that the final vision statement is well grounded in reality and practicality, its designers must, as critically and objectively as possible, test it against the standards set by the earlier detailed analyses of future markets, competition, resources, capabilities, and so on.

3. *Although we normally think of visioning as a singularly individual exercise, a well-designed collective visioning process can work.* Each approach has its pros and cons. Intuitively, we can see that a charismatic leader is most likely to arrive at, and articulate, a personal vision of where he or she wants to lead the company. This approach has the advantage of simplicity, at least in the formative stage, and promotes forcefulness and consistency, given that only one person drives the process.

Individual visioning does, however, present some problems. Seldom can a single mind supply all the necessary insights to produce a vision that is complete, realistic, and challenging. Truly penetrating insights most frequently come from the interplay—indeed, the friction (in a benign sense)—between different perspectives. But, even if this were not the case, the leader needs to build understanding, consensus, and commitment from the first day, starting with the senior management team. An individual vision may not begin with a cadre of collegial support. Indeed, frequently a vision challenges conventional thinking, and colleagues are the first people the visionary must persuade to the new point of view. If they do not come around, the danger of backlash and undermining of the vision is high.

The arguments against collective visioning are generally mirror images of those just cited. Diversity of experience and perspectives improves the chances of achieving a complete and rounded vision. The danger of backlash diminishes, and the communication process starts with a cadre of committed supporters, each prepared to carry the torch to the broader corporate audience. This process can also foster the teamwork that is critical in today's complex environment and may be particularly useful when a new management team is forming. The key pitfall is one that awaits any form of consensus building: consensus often emerges only from compromise, and compromise may so weaken the final product that it ceases to be visionary.

Over the years, I have consulted on collective visioning projects with executives from diverse industries and nationalities. In nearly every case, the strategic vision was not the sole focus of the project. Rather, it was an element—in many cases, the capstone—in a larger strategic study. Typically, this collective approach has involved the whole senior management team in a series of workshops, with extensive intervening staff support. These factors probably helped to ground the vision better in strategic thinking, and to gain it broader and more forthcoming support, because it was less likely to be perceived as a blue-sky exercise.

Certainly, the collective process does work. It works in the fundamental and important sense of developing a dynamic and usable product. It provides a framework (not a straitjacket) within which differing perspectives and values and different types of thinking (analytical, creative) can be integrated and accommodated. And the pace allows time for reflection and second thoughts without losing the momentum needed to keep the project alive.

4. *Considerable value can be added by the judicious use of diverse contributions, including those of informed outsiders.* Visioning is, necessarily, a values-laden, emotional process, so in the final analysis, the determinative input must be that of insiders—those who will be charged with responsibility for implementing the vision. However, outsiders can still be called upon to make valuable contributions in the form of their knowledge of markets, competitors, and technology—and even their (hopefully) more objective assessment of the company itself.

5. *Finally, and most importantly, the CEO must be the driving force behind any vision.* Probably the most successful efforts originate in the mind of one individual who then hones the vision as he or she builds consensus in the senior management team before "going public." (This was certainly the approach taken by Carly Fiorina as she strove to

execute her vision of a combined Hewlett Packard–Compaq.) But even a collective approach to visioning must derive its power from the approval and participation of the CEO. In the final analysis, the choice of approach must reflect the management style of the CEO and the organizational culture of the company.

CHARACTERISTICS OF A SUCCESSFUL VISION

Having a detailed strategic vision does not, of course, guarantee success. Nor does the lack of vision necessarily mean failure. A sound strategic vision is, however, one more weapon in the competitive arsenal of today's corporation—one that could add enough thrust and cutting edge to allow a company that is merely muddling through to transform itself into a vigorous competitor.

Analyzing the visions of Welch, Carlzon, and others and drawing on my own experience lead me to conclude that there are five characteristics that successful visions share: clarity, coherence, communications power, consistency, and—surprisingly perhaps—flexibility.

Clarity

A clear vision is, in part, a simple one. Often, complex analyses lie behind seemingly simple statements of vision—Welch's vision is a prime case in point—but to generate understanding, support, and commitment, the vision statement should be clear and relatively simple, emphasizing basic principles and driving forces.

Clarity helps guide the strategy and derives its power as much from what the vision statement cuts out (the consumer electronics business in GE's case, for example) as from what it includes. It does not aim for all-embracing, motherhood-type concepts, or to be all things to all people. It imposes a clear sense of direction, priorities, and strategy.

Coherence

A successful vision statement makes sense. It is both internally consistent (the pieces of the vision fit together) and consistent with market and competitive conditions (the vision has a reasonable chance of being achieved, given the probable future that the business faces). This coherence is vital if the vision is to stand up to critical analysis. A coherent vision helps a company endure through changes in the real world and helps persuade employees to commit themselves to its execution.

Communications Power

If a vision is to shape the corporate future and drive strategy, then the CEO and other executives must communicate it broadly, consistently, and continuously until it becomes an accepted part of the corporate culture. And the vision itself must have communications power—forcefulness, memorability, and simplicity. For 20 years, Welch took every public and corporate opportunity—in speeches, writings, management meetings, and interviews—to drive home his message, hammering at the basic need for change, interpreting the basic principles in terms that his audience could understand, enriching the vision with new initiatives, and encouraging a gung-ho commitment to its realization.

Indeed, it is only through communication that the vision can become a shared vision—one that stimulates action throughout the organization—though it takes much more than communication to make the sharing complete.

Consistency

If actions speak louder than words, then corporate decisions and actions must be—and people must perceive them to be—consistent with the vision statement. A good visionary knows this intuitively: the intent must always be to practice, in every corporate decision and action (Carlzon's "moments of truth," for example), what the vision preaches. Welch was always sensitive to charges of inconsistency in some of his decisions (for example, the swap of consumer electronics for Thomson's medical diagnostics) but was able to meet the charges of opportunism by referring to the often stated principles of his vision.

Flexibility

A vision must remain flexible and open. A flexible vision may seem to be an oxymoron because a vision calls for defined direction and goal seeking, whereas flexibility implies a more opportunistic approach to strategy. The truth is, however, that in times of high uncertainty, strategy must be open to new signals of change, alert to the possible need for changes in tactics and approach, and flexible enough even to consider redefining the vision. Inflexible adherence to a strategic plan is a prescription for disaster. Flexibility need not mean abandoning the vision: it simply recognizes the need to tune the vision continually to an ever-changing business environment.

REALIZING THE POWER OF VISION

As with anything as sensitive and atypical of normal corporate behavior as vision, there is a host of pitfalls and barriers to successful implementation. Among the more significant, I would count executive impatience (as was the case with my CEO friend cited at the beginning of this chapter); a failure of imagination, coupled with a willingness to go along with the conventional; a failure to build consensus around the vision; lack of flexibility in execution; and, quite simply, a failure to implement, leaving the vision as nothing more than a statement of good intentions. Yet, despite these problems, the rewards that come from realizing the power of vision are great enough to merit serious and persistent effort to make vision an integral element of corporate culture and behavior.

As the encapsulated and (hopefully) inspiring image of "what we want to be (and can be)," vision can be a powerful force in implementing strategy. It focuses corporate thought and action on the agreed-upon strategy, helping to ensure that everyone marches to the same drummer—not in any rigid, conformist sense, for we need to encourage individual thought and initiative; but to ensure that we all march in the same direction, adhering to a common set of values and objectives. It provides both the readiness and the aim—as in, "ready, aim, fire"—for both strategic and operational decisions, thereby helping to ensure consistency throughout the decision-making process. This factor is most important, not merely in strategic decisions, but in tactical decisions when, as managers point out, little or no time is available for detailed analysis before taking action. But if managers have internalized a well-thought-through vision, aim is ever present in their minds to guide their decision making.

Developing a vision helps a company improve its effectiveness by increasing employees' understanding of strategic objectives and motivating their performance in conformity with these objectives. Although developing a vision incurs a cost in executive time, it requires marginal extra effort and is a cost well worth incurring. For perhaps 5 to 10 percent extra effort (in addition to the time executives would normally spend developing strategy), integrating this work into a coherent strategic vision increases the overall effectiveness of the effort as much as 50 percent and probably doubles the chances that managers and employees alike will rally behind the strategy.[8]

By dramatically contrasting a picture of the company of the future with the present reality, strategic vision helps convey the extent of the total internal changes that the organization must make—and the reasons for them. Of course, this is not the only way to win an understanding of change, but it is a valuable by-product of visioning, particularly because it treats the corporation, and the effect of change, as a whole, avoiding the pitfalls of the usual piecemeal approach.

The payoff for strategic vision is more than a reputation for business statesmanship. Vision translates directly into improved customer satisfaction, sustained competitive advantage, greater employee commitment, and increased shareowner value. We need only look at *Fortune*'s list of "America's Most Admired Corporations" for corroborating evidence. What is necessary to win—and keep—such a reputation? Certainly, consistently high profitability is one key to success; the link between reputation and shareowner value is strong. And, more often than not, a strong visionary leader heads the corporation: Bill Gates of Microsoft, Herb Kelleher of Southwest Airlines, Michael Dell of Dell Computers, Andy Grove of Intel, the late Sam Walton of Wal-Mart, and Welch of GE. One can make a similar list of business leaders, past and present, in other nations—Akio Morita, of Sony; Percy Barnevik, of ABB Asea Brown Boveri and now Investor; Soichico Honda, of Honda Motors; and Carlzon, of SAS—who have leveraged vision to business success.

As such leaders have shown, strategic vision can empower employees to act differently, change the way the corporation operates and relates to its stakeholders, and help the company move toward a long-term goal. This achievement is corporate renewal in a most profound and continuing sense.

The historian Arnold Toynbee interpreted human history as a series of challenges and responses. In the corporate world, strategic vision both provides the challenge and lights the way to the needed response. The lesson of history is never to let the vision lapse: always renew, always challenge, always empower.

NOTES

1. *The New Webster Encyclopedic Dictionary of the English Language* (1980), s.v. "vision."

2. Ibid.

3. As in much of this book, I have chosen to focus on corporate experience and examples, in part because that is where most of my experience lies, but also because the best known and most powerful examples are to be found in this arena. I should stress, however, that both the basic concept, and many of the details of its approach, can be successfully applied in other types of organizations such as universities, health care facilities, community welfare organizations, and other not-for-profit organizations.

4. We must recognize that not every vision can be equally inspiring—not, that is, if it is realistic. Not every company can enjoy the exciting and dynamic possibilities of a GE. In some cases, the vision may even be limiting in the sense, that is, of focusing a corporation on its core competencies and most achievable markets and sources of competitive advantage.

5. For a historic record of the evolution of Welch's vision, and for further details on its key elements, I suggest that the reader review his series of letters to share owners in the company's Annual Reports, starting in 1983. They are unique in management literature (let alone in the usually staid field of annual reports) for their clarity of thinking, their informal and hard-hitting messages, and the perspective they provide on the evolution of this vision over a 20-year period.

6. Benjamin B. Tregoe and John W. Zimmerman, *Top Management Strategy: What It Is and How to Make It Work* (New York: Simon and Schuster, 1980). See especially chapter 3 of their book, "Driving Force and the Nine Basic Strategic Areas."

7. See chapter 3, the section "The Attributes of Strategic Management," where I define it as "running the business on the basis of a coherent vision of what the business can and should be. . . . "

8. This estimate is, of course, illustrative, and is based on the assumption that the senior executive team engages in a collective visioning exercise similar to that outlined earlier in this chapter.

Chapter 6

STRATEGY IN UNCERTAIN TIMES

"We shall never be able to escape from the ultimate dilemma that all our knowledge is about the past, and all our decisions are about the future."
My presentation to the American Association for the Advancement of Science, 1975[1]

If developing a vision and harnessing the power of opposites are two of the subtle elements in strategy, dealing with uncertainty is most assuredly another.

For the past 40 years we have lived in a world of growing complexity and accelerating change. It has been an age to which, in an effort to make our world more comprehensible (if not more comfortable), we have given a variety of labels—"an era of radical change," "the postindustrial society," "the Information Age," "the Globalized Society," and the ill-fated "New Economy." It is in the confluence of these forces that the future lies; and it will, almost inevitably, be a future of turbulence and uncertainty. As the futurist Alvin Toffler has noted: "The changes we are going through are much bigger than dot. coms and digitization. We are shifting to a knowledge-based economy, and one should not expect unbroken growth. Expect turbulence, surprises, chance. That's what revolution brings." Turbulence and uncertainty have become the "new normalcy" of our lives.

PLANNING AND UNCERTAINTY

Each of the labels we have put on the future has captured some particular aspect of the multiple revolutions now playing out on the world stage. And, collectively, the trends that they describe constitute the fabric of our present and probable future world. As such, they are useful tools for our analyses and communication.

However, from the point of view of planning and strategy, the dominant characteristic of our times—the one that pervades each one of these forces and largely influences the way we look at the world—is uncertainty. Throughout history, there has always been an inevitable element of uncertainty about the future; but it has been vastly magnified over the past century by the increasing pace, complexity, and interconnectedness of change. Now it is woven inextricably into the whole fabric of the future. (See, for example, Nortel's attempt at spelling out the range of uncertainties that it has to confront in its planning—Box 6.1.)

Uncertainty is something other than risk, with which business and many other organizations are familiar. With risk, you can assign various probabilities to events you know may occur. With uncertainty, you know that you don't know what may occur. Stated another way, it is virtually certain that things will go wrong (i.e., against predictions) at least as often as they go right.

Despite this fact, however, there seems to be a very human drive, particularly among business executives, toward forecasting, a refusal to give up on prediction. The crystal ball is more than a cartoon symbol of our striving to know the future. It literally represents our trust in the expert (the gypsy) and her arcane power of knowing (the crystal). We would be well advised to remember the old saying: "Those who live by the crystal ball are doomed to die from eating broken glass!"

There is a strong cultural taproot reaching deep into early human history and our primal desire to reduce, and if possible eliminate, uncertainty. And, while that concern was originally focused primarily on the present, it gradually and naturally extended into the future. Driven by self-preservation, a natural inquisitiveness, and a somewhat arrogant presumption as to their supremacy in the natural order, humans in most cultures (particularly Western) have developed a compulsion to know. Knowing meant reducing uncertainty, it made the world seem more ordered and orderly, and it signified competence, control, and security.

This very human trait manifests itself most strongly among planners and managers. The planning culture in most corporations is still biased toward single-point forecasting. In this context, the manager's premise

---

Box 6.1
Nortel Confronts Uncertainty

In the wake of the collapse of the telecommunications market in 2000–2001, Nortel Networks engaged in a comprehensive assessment of the full range of uncertainty that confronted the company in its strategic planning. The results of this assessment were included in a major section of the company's 2001 Annual Report, detailing the extent of the uncertainties that investors should consider when evaluating the "forward-looking statements" contained in this report.

Some of these uncertainties derive from internal factors such as possible difficulties in implementing restructuring initiatives, an inability to attract or retain specialized technical and managerial personnel, and difficulties in integrating strategic alliances into the company's culture and structure. But the critical uncertainties—those over which the company has no control—revolve around the volatility and changes in the complex environment in which the company operates For example:

- Economic conditions in the United States and Canada, and globally
- Rationalization and consolidation in the telecoms industry and consequent loss of customers
- Changes in strategy and structure among the company's customers
- Future levels of spending on telecommunications infrastructure
- Volatility arising from changing technologies, evolving industry standards, new product introductions, and short product life cycles
- Uncertainties in international trade, such as trade protection measures, exchange controls, currency fluctuations, and nationalization of local industry
- Regulation of the Internet (e.g., regarding encryption and access charges)

In sum, then, there is virtually no aspect of the company's environment that is not fraught with a high degree of volatility and uncertainty.

---

is, "Tell me what the future will be; then I can make my decision." This premise is reinforced by the way we define managerial competence. Good managers know where they are, know where they're going, and know how they'll get there. In other words, we equate managerial competence with knowing and assume that decisions depend on facts about the present and about the future. Of course, the reality is that we have no absolute facts about the future. As I said in my address to the AAAS (American Association for the Advancement of Science), everything we truly know relates to the past (or possibly the present). Our knowledge—strictly defined—does not and cannot extend to the future.

Faced with this dilemma, planners have turned to a variety of methodologies and approaches in an effort to get some grip on the future.

Conceptually, there are three approaches that executives can take to the problem of uncertainty.

The first choice, and the one most favored by managers and planners, is to adopt a so-called sledgehammer approach to the problem: gathering more data, developing new forecasting methodologies, and devoting more and more resources to solving the problem, in an effort to enhance the accuracy of their forecasting capabilities. However, while it is commendable that we should try to improve our understanding of what is happening (and likely to happen) in our world, the ultimate objective of being able to predict the future will almost certainly remain elusive, and probably unattainable. And, in a turbulent and uncertain environment, single-point forecasts are inherently inaccurate, and strategies based on them will almost certainly be misdirected.

Alternatively, we can give up on the problem of trying to predict the future, arguing that forecasting in such a turbulent environment is doomed to failure, and so the best we can do is set our course, monitor the present (what is actually happening), and be flexible enough to respond to the inevitable changes that the future will bring. But, while flexibility is a highly desirable and indeed necessary trait in these conditions, it gives no sense of direction and purpose. It cannot, in and of itself, be a strategy.

The third approach is to steer a middle course between deluding ourselves as to the accuracy of our forecasts and giving up on thinking about the future entirely. After all, some things about the future are more or less predictable because they have already occurred, but their consequences have not yet unfolded. A prime example of such a forecast is the future size of population age groups as cohorts pass through predictable age brackets—the so-called pig in a python phenomenon. We have thus been able to predict the successive impacts of the baby boom generation as they passed through their life stages of school, college, marriage, employment, promotion, and retirement.

Identifying such predetermined elements is important and fundamental to serious planning, but seldom, if ever, are there enough of them to constitute a complete single-point forecast. There are always residual uncertainties that must be taken into account in developing strategy. As Pierre Wack, Royal Dutch/ Shell's planning guru during the 1970s, used to stress:

Decision makers facing uncertain situations have a right to know just how uncertain they are. Accordingly, it is essential to try to put as much light on critical uncertainties as on the predetermined elements. They should not be swept under the carpet.[2]

The inevitable consequence of this fact is that strategy should be the product not of a single-point forecast but of a set of alternative futures that explore these uncertainties.

And that is where scenarios come into play.

SCENARIOS: A MATTER OF DEFINITION

What do I mean by "scenarios"? In simple, colloquial terms, we can think of them as "stories of possible futures." And certainly this definition is accurate in at least two respects. Scenarios are stories in the sense that they describe the evolving dynamics of interacting forces rather than the static picture of a single end-point future (see Box 6.2). And the futures that they describe are possible and plausible; they are not posed as hypothetical extremes—utopia and dystopia.

A more complete definition fleshes out these ideas and starts to define the uses to which scenarios can be put in the strategy process: "Scenarios are frameworks for structuring executives' perceptions about alternative future environments in which their decisions might be played out." Each element in this definition has a particular significance in scenarios' relationship to strategy:

Box 6.2
Scenarios: What They Are and Are Not

Scenarios Are Not	They Are
Predictions	Descriptions of alternative plausible futures
Variations around a midpoint base case	Significantly, often structurally, different views of the future
Snapshots of end-points (e.g., the market in 2010)	Movies of the evolving dynamics of the future
Generalized views of feared or desired futures	Specific decision-focused views of the future
Product of outside futurists	Result of management insight and perceptions

Scenarios are frameworks for structuring . . .

In the strategy context, scenarios—like vision—have a specific, purposeful meaning. They are not loosely developed fictions but structured explorations of the future that strategy will have to deal with. The structure needs to be tight enough to give discipline, coherence, and relevance to the final product, but loose enough to be able to embrace the creative, and sometimes unconventional, insights of the executives and planners who will use the scenarios. (It is not my intention here to describe the scenario development process in detail, but the case study in Appendix D will give the interested reader an overview of one approach to developing scenarios for use in strategy.)

. . . executives' perceptions . . .

Because the scenarios are intended to be used as a key framework for strategy development, it is vitally important that they should reflect the thinking of the executives who will ultimately be responsible for developing and executing the strategy. This should not be taken to mean that the scenarios should simply reflect the current conventional thinking in the organization about the future. Indeed, as Pierre Wack insisted, scenarios should be designed to challenge, rather than reinforce, executives' "mental maps of the way the world works." But it does mean that the decision makers should understand and accept the reasoning that led to the development and selection of the scenarios if they are to have sufficient confidence in the final product to use it in their strategic thinking. Executive ownership of the scenarios is, thus, a sine qua non for their effective use.

. . . about alternative future environments . . .

The emphasis here is on the plural—alternative futures. To cover what we might term "the envelope of acknowledged uncertainty," we need a set of scenarios. How many? That depends on many things including the scope and complexity of the arena covered by the scenarios and executives' tolerance for uncertainty and ambiguity. However, as a general rule, a set of two to four scenarios is usually sufficient to cover the envelope of uncertainty and act as test beds for strategy development. Any number above this range tends to become unwieldy and counterproductive.

. . . in which their decisions might be played out.

Although it is, of course, possible to develop scenarios on a broad topic such as "The Future of the Globalized Economy," scenarios that are to be used in the strategy development process should be more decision focused—that is, they need to focus on the key trends and forces that will shape the future environment that the strategy must address. In the Statoil case cited in Appendix D, for example, the scenarios focused on one strategic decision—the technology strategy for the group's Exploration and Production Division—and three critical axes of uncertainty:

- *The structure of the energy market (supply and demand).* Will there be a return to a seller's market, or will the (then current) buyer's market continue?

- *The Norwegian economy.* Will the economy continue to be heavily energy dependent, or will it successfully restructure into a more diversified form?

- *Technology.* Will technology evolve, in the general economy and in energy industries, in a fragmented and somewhat incremental manner, or will a more integrated and accelerated evolution take place?

By and large, this approach to scenarios can be said to have all the strengths and all the limitations of a model that depends on the working of the human brain (or collection of brains). While it may be, for instance, weak on detailed quantification, it has the inestimable strength of capturing the power of both logic and imagination to create stories of the future. And it has the further advantage of its ability to shape both the formal and the informal aspects of the planning system simultaneously.

Of course, other methodologies are available, among them Delphi studies, trend analysis, cross-impact analysis, game theory, and computer-based models of varying sorts. While each approach has its own particular strengths, scenarios have, I believe, some special advantages:

- Because the methodology is relatively simple and completely transparent, it is easy for participants to follow and put into practice.

- The process is highly flexible. It can easily be adapted to the needs of individual situations and indeed uses a specific management decision as the focus and starting point for the whole process. This it can do more easily because it is not dependent on the structure and requirements of a computer model.

- The process places a premium on the identification and clarification of issues. The logics and structure of the scenarios are, essentially, a construct of the mind (more exactly, the collective mind of the management team). This fact imposes on the team a disciplined need to examine, carefully and critically, every key issue and uncertainty in order to clarify the reasons for differing possible futures.

- Finally, and most important, there is a high degree of ownership of the final product. The scenarios have, quite literally, been created by the management team, rather than by subordinate staff or a computer model, and the resulting sense of ownership is absolutely essential in ensuring that the scenarios are, in fact, used effectively rather than being relegated to file and forget.

LINKING SCENARIOS TO STRATEGY

What do we do with scenarios once we have developed them? How do we translate what we learn from them into action? Before attempting to answer these questions, let me suggest two things that we should not do.

First, we do not develop a complete strategy for each of the scenarios and then by some means—maybe by applying the test of discounted cash flow—select the one that appears to give the greatest promise of success and profitability. I know of no management team that would willingly undertake to go through a full-blown strategy development exercise two or three or four times (however many scenarios have been developed). Such a course would more likely lead to paralysis by analysis than to constructive action.

The second thing that we do not do is to assign probabilities to the scenarios and then develop a strategy for the most probable one. Probability has more to do with forecasts than with scenarios, and scenarios are not forecasts, for one cannot, reasonably and at the same time, forecast three or four quite different futures. Scenarios, as a collection of futures, are intended to establish the boundaries of our uncertainty and the limits to plausible futures.

However, I recognize that there is a very powerful human tendency, born of past experience and culture, to assign probabilities at the end of the scenario process. Every individual on the team ends up with his or her own private assessment of probability; and it is almost certainly better to bring these assessments out into the open for group discussion than to leave them suppressed in individual minds. Indeed, doing this usually serves to underscore the wide diversity of assessments—and the consequent foolishness of trying to reach some sort of consensus on this matter. However, whichever course of action one chooses—to engage in this group assessment or not—the critical point is to avoid playing the probabilities game to the point of focusing on one most probable scenario to the exclusion of others. To do so would negate the whole value of the scenario planning exercise.

Sometimes managers can become so captivated by the excitement of developing scenarios that they forget that these pictures of the future are not an end in themselves: they are a means to help managers make better strategic decisions. But it is precisely at this point of linkage between scenarios and strategy that decision makers seem to have the greatest difficulty. Too often, their response to the completion of the scenarios is an anticlimactic, "Now what?"

In the long run, strategizing within a framework of scenarios is a skill that requires considerable sophistication and takes time to acquire, as Royal Dutch/Shell's experience so clearly demonstrated. But every manager's immediate need is for a utilitarian primer that explains, step by step, how to move from scenarios to strategy. Some will protest that this approach misstates the purpose of scenarios, trivializes strategy development, substitutes analytical structure for intuitive insight, and overlooks other vital inputs to the process. There is some validity to these arguments. However, in defense of this utilitarian approach, I would argue that it is rather like learning to play the piano. The beginner has to learn the notes, play the scales, and play rhythmically, paced by a metronome. Only after mastering these basic techniques can the piano player successfully perform with feeling and insight. So, too, the beginning scenarios player needs to practice some basic techniques that will help to bridge the gap between scenarios and strategy.

What follows are some exemplary techniques that such a primer might contain, ranging from the most elemental to the more sophisticated.

Sensitivity/Risk Assessment

Scenarios can be extremely useful in evaluating a specific strategic decision such as a major plant investment or new business development. In brief, this approach uses computer modeling (with the scenarios providing the underlying assumptions), or simple judgmental assessments, to evaluate the strategy's resilience or vulnerability in a variety of different business conditions.

The steps in such an approach would be the following:

- Identify the key conditions in the future market/industry environment—for example, the size and growth rate of the market, changes in regulatory climate, or technological breakthroughs—that would be necessary for management to make a so-called go decision, that is, if these conditions are met, then a decision to move forward with the investment would be appropriate.

- Describe and assess the state of these conditions in each scenario.

- Compare these scenario conditions with the desired future conditions and evaluate the likely success or failure—and the resilience or vulnerability—of a go decision in each scenario.

- Finally, evaluate the overall resilience or vulnerability of a go decision and assess the desirability of hedging or modifying the original decision in order to increase its resilience.

This approach offers a relatively simple application in a series of descriptive and judgmental steps. It does, however, depend on having a very clear and specific decision focus that lends itself to a relatively straightforward "go/no go" decision.

For example, a paper company needed to decide whether to invest $600 million in a new paper-making facility. The plant would have a long life span (probably some 30 to 35 years) and a relatively narrow range of products, and management had some concern about eventual erosion of the target market because of the advent of electronic transactions. The company, therefore, decided to use scenarios to explore the possible variations in market size and growth rate, given the uncertainties about the pace of future electronic technology developments, consumer values and their use of time, prospects for advertising, and general economic conditions.

The scenarios showed, as one might expect, distinctly different levels of demand growth but similar patterns of eventual decline, with the timing of key threats remaining a critical uncertainty. Playing out the investment decision in these different environments suggested that only in the most optimistic conditions would the company meet its hurdle rate for return on investments. As a result, the executives decided on an incremental approach to the investment, significantly scaling back the initial plant size. Interestingly, too, the scenarios also implied a far higher near-term demand for certain key products than conventional industry wisdom anticipated at the time. The company broke with conventional thinking, increased manufacturing capacity for these products, and reaped significant gains during the following decade when its competitors were unprepared to meet the surge in orders.

Strategy Evaluation

Scenarios can also be useful as test beds to evaluate the viability of an existing or proposed strategy. Since the strategy will usually have derived from a single-point forecast, it is obviously helpful to play the proposed strategy against a set of scenarios in order to assess its effectiveness in a range of business conditions. At the very least, it should then be possible to identify modifications to the strategy that might strengthen it or contingency plans that should be undertaken.

The steps in such an approach would be the following:

- Disaggregate the strategy into its main component parts (e.g., "Focus development on consumer market segments in . . . ," "Build strategic alliances with . . . ," "Diversify into related service areas"), and review stated objectives and goals.
- Assess the relevance, and likely success (or failure), of these thrusts in the diverse conditions of each scenario.
- Analyze the results of this impact analysis in order to identify the following:
  - Opportunities that the strategy addresses and those it misses
  - Threats/risks that the strategy has foreseen or overlooked
  - The comparative competitive success or failure of the strategy in each scenario.
  - Identify the possible options for changes in the strategy and/or the need for contingency planning.

This approach offers a natural way to introduce scenarios into a traditional strategic planning system that has been based on single-point forecasting. While it doesn't make the fullest possible use of scenarios, it does quickly identify bottom-line issues, broaden planners' perspectives, and initiate them into the concept of alternative futures.

A large department store chain introduced scenarios into its strategic planning system as a means of exploring alternative future patterns of change in the economy, consumer values and lifestyles, consumer buying decisions, and the structure and operations of the retail industry. The company then used these scenarios in three ways:

- To evaluate the likely payoff from its current strategy (that is, the projected payoff from each of the key thrusts of its current strategy)
- To assess and compare the strategies of key competitors
- To analyze retail strategy options to identify the most resilient ones for possible inclusion in the company's strategy.

As one result, the company greatly expanded its specialty retail outlets because of the new market understanding it gained from developing the scenarios. As a consequence, it was able to win appreciable market share (and increased profitability) from the then market leader, Sears Roebuck.

Strategy Development (Using a Planning Focus Scenario)

Selecting one scenario as a starting point for strategy development is, in some ways, a distortion of the scenario concept, but, if used carefully, it can accommodate current management culture and make the introduction of scenarios into the system easier and more acceptable. In essence, this approach develops a strategy to deal with the conditions of one scenario and then tests that strategy against the other scenarios to assess its resilience and the need for any modification, hedging, and contingency planning.

The steps in this approach would be the following:

- Review the scenarios to identify strategic opportunities and threats for the business.
- Determine what the company should do, and not do, in any case.
- Select a planning focus scenario (usually the one judged to be the most probable).
- Integrate the product of the preceding steps into a coherent strategy for this scenario.
- Test this strategy against the remaining scenarios to assess its resilience and vulnerability.
- Review the results of this test to determine the need for strategy modification, hedging, and contingency planning.

Clearly, this approach flies in the face of strict scenario theory (by dealing with probabilities), but it can be a useful intermediate step in weaning executives from reliance on single-point forecasts. Certainly, it avoids the pitfall of picking one scenario to the exclusion of others—a fault that would negate the value of scenarios totally. In its step-by-step process, it addresses many key questions that scenario-based strategy should ask. Its major liability, however, is that it can close executive minds to unlikely (or unpleasant) scenarios and in the process limit the search for strategy options.

When Shell Canada introduced scenarios into its strategic planning system in the early 1980s, the company elected to ease into the new process by using this approach. From this initial point, the company built up its corporate strategy from the answer to three questions:

- Which strategies should we pursue no matter which scenario materializes?
- Which strategies should we pursue if the planning focus scenario materializes?
- How sensitive are these base-case strategies to variations in assumptions under contingent conditions (the other scenarios)?

By adopting this approach, Shell Canada tried to bridge the gap between the old and the new strategy development process while preserving the value of considering, and planning for, the contingencies resulting from widely different business conditions.

One outcome of this initial venture into scenario planning was the company's decision to give up on some of its peripheral ventures (into biotechnology, for example) and to concentrate on its resources and chemicals businesses.

Strategy Development (without Using a Planning Focus Scenario)

This approach takes all scenarios at face value, avoiding the trap of assigning probabilities to them. It concentrates on developing a "resilient" strategy that can deal with wide variations in business conditions.

The steps in such an approach would be the following:

- Identify the key elements of a complete strategy—for example, geographic scope, market focus, basis of competition, technology, alliances, and so forth.
- Analyze each scenario to determine the optimum setting for each element (e.g., What would be the best market focus for Scenario A? For Scenario B?).
- Review these scenario-specific settings and determine the most resilient option for each element (e.g., Which market focus would be most best able to cope with the different market conditions in the scenarios?).
- Integrate these options into an overall, coordinated business strategy.

This approach most closely approximates the goal of strategizing within the scenarios framework and so makes optimum use of scenarios in strategy development. It provides management with the maximum feasible range of choice and forces careful evaluation of the options against different futures. However, it makes serious demands on the patience, imagination, and effort of the decision makers involved in the process.

The senior management team of a major Irish bank became both the scenario- and strategy-development team in its review of the bank's strategic direction. After structuring scenarios around their perceptions of the critical uncertainties facing their business, the CEO and his direct reports first identified the strategic opportunities and threats arising from the scenarios and used this framework to assess the bank's current competitive position and prospective vulnerability. Their approach to future strategy then led them through the following steps:

- Single out the elements of a well-rounded strategy (product scope, technology, alliances, and the like).
- Identify the optimal strategy for each of these elements in each of four scenarios.
- Select the most resilient option for each element and integrate these options into a coherent strategy for the bank.

The bank's strategic planning officer credited his company's scenarios with helping to provide a clear and consistent focus for the company's strategy. Since they developed the scenarios, he said, "Reliance on strategic ad-hocracy has diminished."

THE ISSUE OF RESILIENCE

At various points in this chapter I have referred to the need for a resilient strategy, one capable of dealing with the uncertainties of the future as they are represented in the scenarios. However, a word of caution—and explanation—is called for.

It should be obvious that resilience is not the only quality to be sought in a strategy. And, taken to an extreme, resilience could mean little more than the lowest common denominator of scenario-specific strategies. Michael Porter, for one, has argued that this is the fatal flaw in scenario-planning: it inevitably leads to suboptimization of strategic effort and resources. In rebuttal, one might ask, "For which future, then, should we optimize our strategy? Do you want to single out a particular future for which we should prepare and neglect the others?" But, while this might score some debating points, it does not respond effectively to his challenge.

At a time that calls for bold, even radical, action in many markets, taking this interpretation of resilience would be a prescription for mediocrity at best, extinction at worst. In the most general terms, there are at least three options open to those charged with responsibility for selecting strategy. The most aggressive option is a preemptive strike, taking a leadership role in reshaping the way an industry or a market operates, as Dell Computer did when it adopted its direct selling model for the personal computer business. Alternatively, a company can opt for an adaptive posture, relying on its speed and flexibility to seize and exploit opportunities as they arise, as GE has done in its globalization strategy. Or, thirdly, it can select what Hugh Courtney calls "reserving the right to play," making incremental investments today that put the company in a privileged position through superior information, cost structures, or relationships between customers and suppliers.[3] That allows a company to wait until the environment becomes less uncertain before committing itself to a stronger, more definitive strategy.

My point is not to prejudge which option a company should take in any given situation. That choice depends on many factors—management values, risk tolerance, the availability of resources—quite as much as on its assessment of the future. Rather, I would argue that, before taking any steps, whether bold or tentative, the strategy should be tested against a variety of scenarios so that the management team is forewarned of potential vulnerabilities. Resilience can then be built into the strategy, not necessarily by reducing its force or boldness, but by hedging or contingency planning.

In the final analysis, then, resilience is as much a condition of the organization's culture as it is of the strategy per se. And that leads us directly into the next chapter.

NOTES

1. Ian Wilson, "Societal Change and the Planning Process," presented at the AAAS Annual Meeting, New York, 31 January 1975.

2. Pierre Wack, "Scenarios: Uncharted Waters Ahead," *Harvard Business Review,* September–October 1985, 73–89.

3. Hugh Courtney, *20/20 Foresight: Crafting Strategy in an Uncertain World* (Boston: Harvard Business School Press, 2001).

Chapter 7

DEVELOPING A STRATEGIC CULTURE

"Strategy and culture are arguably the most used and abused words
in the business lexicon. So to discuss the creation of a strategic culture
as a source of competitive advantage is inviting trouble."
                    Mike Freedman, president of World-Wide Strategy Practice,
                                                        Kepner-Tregoe[1]

Over the past 20 years or so, "corporate culture" has become, along with
strategy, a standard element in the management lexicon. Before then, the
phrase was more likely to appear in the academic writings of behavioral
scientists than in the planning documents of corporate executives. And
most managers' reaction to any suggestion that their organization had a
culture problem was, typically, to yawn, shake their heads in disbelief,
and suggest that the discussion proceed to more concrete and productive
matters.

A watershed event was Jack Welch's accession to the leadership of
GE in 1981 and his efforts to change not merely the strategy and the
organization, but also the culture of the company. From the outset, he
foresaw both the need for change and the extent of the effort needed to
effect that change. "From my experience," he wrote, "changing strategy
and improving vision are a lot easier than moving culture. I applaud the
advice you have given your customer."[2] Time has proved him right.

Since that time, the ubiquitous emphasis on empowerment, John
Kotter's demonstration of the linkage between corporate culture and per-

formance,[3] Peter Senge's research and writings on the "learning corporation,"[4] and Welch's own driving efforts in this domain have combined to elevate the term to a level of near unquestioning acceptance.

But use can lead to abuse. Too often the term is used as a catch-all phrase, without a full understanding of its meaning, and certainly without an appreciation of the difficulties inherent in any attempt to change a corporate culture.

STRATEGY AND CULTURE

Every organization has a culture: a system of shared assumptions, values, norms, and practices that determine the character of that organization and the behavior of its members. Culture is critical because it is the wellspring of every action that the organization takes. Culture, Mark Youngblood has written, affects every aspect of an organization: ". . . how it is designed, how people relate to one another, what is considered to be true, what is deemed important, the criteria to use for decisions, how to treat customers, and a myriad of other factors."[5]

Culture impacts strategy in at least two ways. It can be an essential element of the strategy itself, and it determines the organization climate that is required for strategic planning and management to take root and flourish.

It is the second aspect of this relationship that I want to explore here. But a brief word about the first aspect is appropriate before passing on. There is a sense in which culture change can be said, in many cases, to *be the strategy*—or at least an important element of it. This was certainly the case with Jack Welch's approach to GE's future. In a very real sense we could say that a critical element of his strategy was to change the culture of the company, as we have already noted—to make it more flexible, entrepreneurial, boundaryless, and responsive to external change (see Box 7.1).

Aligning culture with strategy was also an issue for the German software company SAP, which recognized that, in order to change its strategy, it needed first to change its culture. In its efforts to expand its core business of building the enterprise resource planning (ERP) systems that run customers' "back-office" functions into newer E-business applications, the company recognized that it had to change its own behavior and attitudes toward customers.

In 2000 the company had an internally focused organization built around its core ERP product, with an engineering-driven culture focused on building a single, integrated product that could then be shipped to

---

Box 7.1
GE and Tyco—Culture Counts

In many ways, Tyco International, Ltd., and GE are strikingly similar. Both are unusually diverse in the range of businesses they manage. Both have produced impressive growth rates in recent years, whether by acquisitions or by organic growth. And both have been managed by hard-driving CEOs—Jack Welch and Dennis Kozlowski—each focused on creating steady increases in shareowner value.

But their trajectories seem destined to diverge. While GE has been, and remains, a darling of Wall Street, Tyco's reputation in financial circles has waned. In January 2002 Kozlowski was forced to give up on his efforts to create a model conglomerate from scratch and announce his intention to break up Tyco into four independent companies in an effort to unlock shareowner value.

Part of the explanation for Wall Street's skepticism no doubt lay with analysts' concern over what they perceived as a loss of financial transparency. "Recently," Simon London wrote in the *Financial Times,* "this has been destroying shareholder value faster than Mr. Kozlowski could create it."[6] But even if this skepticism proves to be unfounded, there remains a fundamental difference between the two companies: their culture.

Unlike Tyco, GE's diversity is rooted in history and has thus grown up in a common culture of shared values: even its financial arm, GE Capital, can be traced back to the birth of GE Credit Corporation in the 1930s. Most recently, Welch's emphasis on across-the-company initiatives, boundarylessness, and the sharing of best-in-class business practices have strengthened and broadened these cultural ties. Jeffrey Immelt, Welch's successor as CEO, put it well: "We run a multibusiness company with common cultures, with common management. . . . where the whole is always greater than the sum of its parts. Culture counts."[7]

---

any customer. Part of the company's new approach lay in designing a classic matrix-type organization structure (based on SAP's five major software applications and separate industry groups). But the main change—and challenge—lay in changing the culture from being engineering-centric to business-centric. Wolfgang Kemna, who was appointed to be the new SAP America head about this time, was under no illusion about the scale of the needed change when he made the move to the United States. "It's huge," he said. "We have the technology—the big challenge is with the people."[8]

Changing its internal focus and engineering culture was particularly critical in the United States, where the nature of the market makes the changes even more important. Focusing inward on its ERP platform left SAP vulnerable to the new pressures that the Internet was putting on its customers. So, in one response, SAP located its global marketing not in

Germany, but in New York City's Greenwich Village, and heightened its emphasis on marketing and creativity in branding.

However, there is a broader point to be made here. Regardless of whether culture change is or is not a part of the strategy, companies have to recognize that the very introduction of strategic management into a company requires a change in that organization's culture. Strategic planning and strategic management are not simply new and improved methodologies that can be introduced as easily as many other management tools. Certainly, they require learning new methodologies and new approaches to traditional management responsibilities. But they also imply, and demand, changes in the way members of the organization think about the future and the place of their organization in that future. Strategy begins in the minds of managers, and it is in the mind that this culture shift must begin.

I should point out that this is not just my own opinion: it is reflected in the findings of a survey of corporate issues and practices that I conducted a number of years ago (see Appendix A). Culture clearly headed the array of corporate concerns in the field of strategic management. Virtually every respondent cited some aspect of this challenge, although the interpretation varied considerably from company to company. (Indeed, if one were to include in this category a number of mentions about management culture, which are currently counted under "Management Skills and Commitment" (see Appendix A), the coverage would be nearly 100 percent.) In broad terms, the references to culture fell into one of three categories: problems, general attributes, and specific attributes.

Problems

In some cases, the focus was on undesirable traits that the company needed to remove in order that strategic management operate more effectively. For instance, respondents cited as barriers to change such personal traits as risk aversion, executives' turf concerns, and internal politics, and organizational problems such as bureaucracy, poor communications, and size. These problems are obstacles both to the development and, most particularly, to the implementation of strategy. One interesting observation—which many planners and executives will share—was that an organization is able to change radically only when it confronts a genuine crisis. In the absence of a real emergency, instilling a sense of impending crisis (even an imagined one) might be necessary to shake up corporate inertia.

General Attributes

Underlying respondents' references to the general traits or attributes that strategic management should seek to instill in a corporation were a willingness and ability to respond to change. At the most basic level, the corporate challenge is simply to generate a willingness to respond, quickly and effectively, to change. At the same time, as one respondent pointed out, enough stability must exist within the organization to provide a firm base from which to deal with change. Most individuals become ineffective in a state of total flux, so balancing stability and change becomes a key challenge for the executive intent on any program of "organizational transformation." Several companies mentioned learning and empowerment as important corporate attributes. Given the pace and complexity of change in their business environments, more and more corporations are recognizing the following:

- Planning is more a matter of continuous organizational learning (scanning, interpreting, and adapting to environmental change) than it is of control.

- Corporate response to change can only be sufficiently rapid, flexible, and pervasive if responsibility filters down into and throughout the organization, maximizing employees' involvement and empowering them to take action.

A Japanese corporation used an anthropological analogy in describing the culture shift it saw was necessary. The Japanese culture, they noted, is fundamentally agricultural. What the Japanese need now—and what they are aiming for—is a "mind change to a hunting culture." Whatever the merits of this interpretation of the Japanese culture, the analogy is interesting and provocative, particularly if one focuses on the attributes of a hunting band: relatively small size, independence, mobility, and team orientation. These are indeed some of the key qualities that any organization should seek to cultivate to deal with today's challenges.

Specific Attributes

Not surprisingly, companies cited speed, flexibility, and enthusiasm as more specific attributes that they need to cultivate if strategy is to move from paper to the marketplace. Streamlining the organizational structure can achieve only so much toward these qualities. A change of attitudes—and behavior—must also take place if these attributes are to be embedded in corporate performance. Thus, culture change itself becomes a primary goal of strategic management. That companies recognize this need for change is, in itself, an indicator and an admission of the real magnitude of the effort required to break away from the ingrained internal bias that has characterized corporate bureaucracy for so long.

CHARACTERISTICS OF A STRATEGIC CULTURE

There are clear differences between a strategic culture—one in which strategic thinking, planning, and action are nurtured and supported—and the long-range planning and budgeting model that has characterized corporate planning for much of the 1960–85 period. I have tried to highlight these differences in Box 7.2, looking at the differing assumptions, values, norms, and practices that characterize each culture.

While I recognize that such a graphic treatment tends to exaggerate the differences between these two cultures, there is value in this emphasis for there are clear distinctions that a strategic culture must aim for if it is to be effective. I should also note that this table includes some characteristics that have already been discussed earlier in the text so what follows should be viewed merely as a summary of these traits.

In its basic assumptions, a strategic culture operates more on the principles of an organic model—a natural system with intrinsic capabilities to change, grow, and renew itself—rather than a mechanistic model subject to the law of entropy and dependent on change being driven into the organization from outside. As Youngblood phrases it, in a mechanistic model, "the responsibility of management is to 'fine-tune' the company until it is 'running like a well-oiled machine,'" while in an organic model, the potential for innovation "already exists in the organization and needs only to be evoked, not imposed by omnipotent executives."[9]

A strategic culture also proceeds, as we have already noted, on the assumption that uncertainty is inescapable, that the future cannot be forecast in sufficient detail to select an obvious strategy, and that what is required of an organization is more often a radical transformation, rather than merely incremental change, in its strategy and behavior. With such a model, planning and strategy development work best if they are distributed rather than centralized responsibilities, diffused as inherent qualities throughout the organization.

In its values, strategic culture—with its acceptance of the certainty of uncertainty—prizes learning over knowing and flexibility and change over consistency and order. The late Donald N. Michael was first to note that, as we learn to plan, we must also plan to learn, and that, in this

---

Box 7.2
The Fundamental Cultural Difference

Traditional (Long-Range Planning) Culture	Strategic Culture
Assumptions	
• The future can be forecast	• Uncertainty is inescapable
• Incremental change will suffice	• Radical transformation is needed
• Planning works best if centralized	• Planning works best if distributed
• Mechanistic model	• Organic model
Values	
• Knowing/Minimizing Risk	• Learning/Embracing errors
• Consistency, predictability, order	• Flexibility and change
• Reality (What is)	• Vision (What will/can be)
• Numbers oriented	• Ideas oriented
Norms	
• Hierarchy	• Heterarchy
• Prime concern is control	• Prime concern is adaptation
• Strategy as a given	• Strategy as choice
• Incremental changes	• Stretch goals
Practices	
• Fixed planning calendar	• Planning as an ongoing activity
• Reliance on methodologies	• Emphasis on thinking
• Internal focus (efficiency)	• External focus (responsiveness)

---

effort, we must have the courage to be "error-embracing."[10] By this provocative term, he did not, of course, mean that we should accept, even encourage, foolish mistakes. Rather, his point was that because uncertainty is inherent in our planning, we must learn our way, step by step, into the future, and in that process accept the fact that errors—in the cybernetic sense of deviations from what we had planned—will inevitable occur. We should, therefore, acknowledge that fact by turning errors into learning experiences, making the needed midcourse corrections in our strategies.

Long-range planning focuses primarily on reality (i.e., what is—the current state of the organization's environment) and is heavily numbers oriented, primarily because of its origins in accounting and heavy emphasis on budgets. Strategic planning, on the other hand, is more concerned with vision (i.e., what can be) and ideas because the environment it has to deal with demands imagination, innovation, and creativity in the strategies that the organization adopts. As a result, strategic culture has what are usually thought of as softer values, ones not normally associated with tightly structured organizations.

The norm or model for such an organization is typically a hierarchy, a multilayered structure of management with centralized authority, designed primarily to control operations. A strategic culture, on the other hand, is heterarchical and polycentric, designed primarily to ensure timely and appropriate adaptation to external changes. Planning and decision-making authority has to be widely diffused throughout the organization because the speed and complexity of today's business environment demand a corresponding speed and flexibility in an organization's response. Strategy, therefore, becomes a distributed capability throughout the organization.

There is, too, a fundamental difference between the two cultures in their perceptions of the need for stretch in strategy. In the traditional planning culture, there seems to be an innate tendency to view continuation of the existing strategy as a given (or, certainly, as the preferred course), driven by the past, and subject only to incremental changes. In a strategic planning culture, however, there is a presumption in favor of the need for change and a far greater willingness to view strategy as a choice among alternatives driven by the future and that demand considerable stretch in the goals set by the organization.

Finally, we can note differences in the planning practices of the two cultures. Most notable is the difference in perceptions about the planning calendar. Traditionally, there is a set schedule of planning sessions—from strategy to operational planning to budgeting, for instance—what Gary Hamel terms the annual rain dance of planning. As Robert Fry, one-time planning officer for Gould, Inc., once put it humorously, but accurately: We strategize in the spring and plan in the fall—and papers flourish and fall like leaves on both occasions. Such an emphasis on adhering to an internal schedule rather than responding to external pressures would be laughable if it were not so serious. Of course, some form of scheduling is needed to ensure that all the planning bases are covered: even as free a spirit as Jack Welch adhered closely to his Sessions A, B, and C and so on.[11] Similarly, we need to use tried and true methodologies in our planning. However, as we have seen, it is when scheduling and methodology become the master rather than the servant of planning that trouble arises.

THE CHALLENGE OF CULTURE SHIFT

In total, these differences between the traditional planning culture and a strategy-oriented culture add up to a culture shift of the first magnitude. And making this shift presents executives with a major challenge. Just how great this challenge is can be gauged by looking again at scenario planning, which is a key element—but still only a part—of the overall strategy culture.

Scenarios, as we have seen, are both more and less than we might expect. They are less than the complete answer to environmental analysis: scanning and monitoring make up the other two legs of the tripod—and even old-fashioned single-point forecasting still has a role to play. But they are also more of a challenge than most people anticipate when they try to integrate scenarios into the planning and decision-making culture of the corporation. Indeed, the two greatest challenges that beginners (and even some old-timers) confront are finding truly effective ways to use scenarios and changing the corporate culture to make it fully compatible with scenarios thinking.

Changing the culture is clearly a more complex and demanding problem than developing the scenarios or ensuring that they are linked to specific strategic decisions. Shell International is probably the premier example in the world of the effective integration of scenarios into planning processes and executive thinking. But the company achieved this happy state only with effort and over time. Pierre Wack began experimenting with scenarios in the early 1970s, just before the first oil shock. Although he quickly gained management's attention as the logic of oil pricing turned upside down in 1973 and 1974, action followed much more slowly. Some five or six years passed before the Committee of Managing Directors felt comfortable using scenarios in its decision making and progress in diffusing scenario planning into the operating companies took even more time. Even now, the spread of scenarios into the Group's global network is uneven and incomplete.

Why do companies, even those who are sincere and persistent in their efforts, have such a hard time in making scenario planning work? No doubt, there are many explanations for this difficulty, but the fundamental problem, I am convinced, is largely a cultural and psychological one.

Most corporate cultures are still heavily biased toward single-point forecasting and quantitative analysis with its emphasis on precision to three decimal places. Scenarios, by contrast, are primarily qualitative products (although quantification of key parameters is needed to give dimension to the story lines), and their emphasis is more on ranges of

possibilities than on precision forecasting. The initial management reaction to them is, therefore, one of suspicion that scenarios are little
better than blue-sky visioning with little relevance and insufficient detail
for strategic planning.

As we have already noted, most corporate decision making is based
on single-point forecasting and the managerial premise, "Tell me what
the future will be, then I can make my decision." Scenarios, by contrast,
are a form of multiple-point exploration and force everyone involved in
the process to view the future and decision making in terms of alternatives. Not surprisingly, managers typically react that, for instance, four
forecasts are more confusing than helpful (never mind that scenarios are
not forecasts), and that alternatives are more appropriate for options than
for futures.

Then, too, managerial competence is normally defined in terms of
knowing. Scenarios, by contrast, confront us with the need to admit that
we do not, and cannot, know the future. To that extent, scenarios seem
to force us to acknowledge some degree of incompetence. And, since
few corporate cultures reward displays of incompetence, managers have
a vested interest in not acknowledging what they don't know.

Add up all these difficulties and barriers, and we can see that the
only way we can hope to remove the old cultural barriers and instill the
new cultural values is through a sustained and comprehensive "transition program" composed of leadership, communication, education, and
measurement.

CREATING A STRATEGIC CULTURE

In his book, *The Corporate Culture Survival Book*,[12] Edgar Schein
makes the important point that any major change in an organization's
culture involves a process of destruction (displacing the old way of doing
things) as well as creation (developing the new) (see Box 7.3). The old
way of doing things—in this case, the values and procedures of traditional long-range planning—is normally so well entrenched, and its ad-
vocates have such a vested interest in its continuation, that its inertia
will defy any but the most determined assault to displace it. The transition has, therefore, to be ought on two fronts simultaneously.

Leadership

I know of no instance of an organization being transformed into a
strategic culture without the active participation—indeed, the drive and

---

Box 7.3
Schein's Three-Stage Model of Transformative Change

Edgar H. Schein, professor emeritus at MIT's Sloan School of Management, argues that any major organizational change has to pass through three phases if it is to take root and flourish as "the new way of doing things around here." If we underestimate the deep sociological and psychological dynamics involved in such a change, he argues, we cannot grasp why culture change is so difficult in organizational midlife, or why it takes so many years.

Stage one involves unlearning the old way of doing things and creating the motivation and drive to change. There has to be some crisis or a sense of dissatisfaction with the old if a drive toward the new is to gather momentum.

In stage two, the emphasis shifts to learning new concepts and new meanings for old concepts. Critical elements in this phase are formal training in the new skills, the formation of support groups, and the identification and imitation of role models.

Finally, stage three focuses on internalizing the new concepts and incorporating them into ongoing relationships. Organizational structures and reward systems must be reviewed and, if need be, revised to ensure that they are consistent with the new way of working.

---

insistence—of its leader. This is scarcely surprising since culture is a critical part of strategy, and strategy is a prime responsibility of leadership. This is true even though, as I have argued, strategic thinking and action should be a distributed capability throughout the organization. It is the leader—the CEO or SBU general manager—who should articulate the vision, communicate the strategy, set the tone for the organization, and, by personal example, show that a truly strategic culture demands the personal involvement of the whole management team. Merely announcing an intention to engage in strategic planning and delegating responsibility to a newly appointed planning executive will not suffice.

The personal example set by the leader is critical because—let's face it—what the CEO wants, the CEO gets. And the signals as to what the CEO wants come from actions more than from words. Protestations about a new beginning that emphasizes a strategic outlook fade into insignificance if, for example, the questioning at planning review sessions focuses on what might be termed short-term incrementalism (next year's budget) rather than vision, on internal requirements rather than external needs. Emerson said it most eloquently: "What you are stands over you the while, and thunders so that I cannot hear you say to the contrary."[13]

So, if an organization is truly serious about culture change, its leaders must embody this change in the way they conduct themselves. They must embrace the values of the new culture so thoroughly, so convincingly, that others will come to see that it is not only an acceptable way to behave: it is the right and necessary way.

Communication

This does not mean, however, that communication is unimportant. On the contrary, it has a vital role to play as a change mechanism. Leadership behavior alone will not suffice: without explanation, it would, at best, lead only to mimetic behavior ("Monkey see, monkey do") rather than true understanding. The greater the change, the greater the need for communication—for clarifying as well as announcing; for discussion as well as exposition; for informal, personal communication as well as formal, written documents; and for repetition as well as elaboration.

Jack Welch was not only the embodiment of the culture shift that he propounded: he was its prime communicator. Throughout his 20-year tenure as CEO of GE, he never let up on his efforts to drive home not only the corporate strategy, but also the culture change that it required. He never missed an audience or an opportunity to communicate the need for—and the nature of—the changes that he was trying to drive into the organization. Inside or outside the company, whether with employees, general managers, or his board of directors, with share owners or financial analysts, with his fellow CEOs or a Harvard Business School class, he hammered away not only on his strategy but on the changes in culture that would be needed to make it succeed. As the strategic initiatives changed, so did his message on the changes in attitude and mindset that the strategy would entail (see Box 7.4). Globalization would require a more open and inclusive international mindset; service and Six-Sigma, a keener sensitivity and flexibility to serve customers and ensure quality; E-business or digitization, a new perspective on relationships with both suppliers and customers along the whole value chain and a new perspective on "learning" as the key source of competitive advantage. And always, of course, there was the need for speed, simplicity, and self-confidence.

To get a better feeling for the range and sensitivity of Welch's communication skills, read his chairman's messages in 20 years of annual reports. These articulate and remarkable documents, so different from the sterile numbers-only reports from most CEOs, are enlightening communiques from the battle front, documenting the evolution of Welch's thinking, values, strategy, and initiatives.

Box 7.4
GE's Initiatives and Culture Change

During his tenure as GE's chairman and CEO, Welch sparked four companywide initiatives in an effort to capture the benefits of new opportunities that changing times presented. These initiatives would, he felt, change not only the scope and scale of the company's businesses, but its culture, the way it conducts itself.

The following excerpt is taken from his chairman's message in the company's 2000 annual report:

Globalization has transformed a heavily U.S,-based Company to one whose revenues are now 40% non-U.S. Even more importantly, it has changed us into a Company that searches the world, not just to sell or to source, but to find intellectual capital: the world's best talents and greatest ideas.

A *Services* focus has changed GE from a Company that in 1980 derived 85% of its revenues from the sale of products to one that today is based 70% on the sale of services. This extends our market potential and our ability to bring value to our customers.

Six Sigma has turned the Company's focus from inside to outside, changed the way we think and train our future leaders and moved us toward becoming a truly customer-focused organization.

. . . . *Digitization* is transforming everything we do, energizing every corner of the Company and making us faster, leaner and smarter even as we become bigger . . .

The initiatives are playing a critical role in changing GE, but the most significant change in GE has been its transformation into a *Learning Company* . . . .

In a truly strategic culture, communication must be two-way—bottom-up and top-down—if we are to achieve the full measure of learning and flexibility that such a culture requires. (Indeed, we could say that it should be *three*-way communication, including the lateral sharing of ideas and best practices that marks a boundaryless organization.) Despite his hard-driving, assertive nature, Welch recognized this fact and, whether in planning sessions or informal meetings, encouraged a free exchange of ideas, a "wallowing" (his word) in information and ideas before arriving at a decision. "It was," he said, "all about breaking down the concept of hierarchy."[14]

Education

Although there is a conventional belief that adults learn more effectively and more quickly by doing than by classroom learning, there is a limited, but important, place for formal education in facilitating this culture shift. This learning experience has to cover not only new procedures and new methodologies for planning, but—far more difficult—new ways of thinking, new priorities, even new values. It must not be merely a matter of rote learning, but of exploration, with one's peers, of new concepts and the intellectual foundation on which they are built. Only then can the validation and elaboration of this learning take place in the work environment.

One company with a long record of building educational bridges to span the culture gaps caused by major changes in organizational structure or theory is GE. Back in the 1950s, the company acquired the estate of Harry Arthur Hopf (one of this country's original management consultants) and established its renowned Manager Development Institute at Crotonville, New York. The original purpose of the Institute was to teach the principles of professional management to the hundreds of managers on whom GE's decentralization program was placing broader and more demanding responsibilities. Then in the early 1970s, when Reginald ("Reg") Jones, then CEO, introduced strategic planning and reorganized the company around SBUs, the changes were accompanied by a sweeping educational program, including two-week courses for soon-to-be strategic planners, shorter courses for all corporate officers and general managers, and half-day on-site briefings for virtually all white-collar staff.

Finally, with the accession of Welch to the top spot, Crotonville was renovated and reoriented to leadership development. The Institute became, in effect, the incubator of reform, a place to spread new ideas in an open give-and-take environment. At the time Welch was severely criticized for spending more than $25 million on building a new guest house and conference center at the same time he was engaged in drastic cost cutting elsewhere. In his autobiographical *Jack: Straight from the Gut,* in a chapter entitled, "Remaking Crotonville to Remake GE," he explained that he wanted to create a place with the right atmosphere where he could instill the values that he wanted spread around the whole company.

Measurement

If there is a golden rule for achieving culture change in an organization, it is surely, "What you would change, measure." Managers, particularly those in corporate settings, are, on the whole, rational beings who will respond to the signals emanating from the organization's nervous system. I wrote earlier that "what the CEO wants, the CEO gets:"

and the clearest signal as to what the CEO wants comes from the management measurement and reward system.

So, if you want to develop a strategic culture, as I describe it here, you must first make clear what the values, norms, and practices of strategic behavior are (see Box 7.2) and then ensure that managerial performance is measured, in part—and then rewarded—against the standards and traits that this culture entails.

In one company that I worked with, the CEO decided that one way to help ensure that strategy was taken seriously and became the new norm for his managers was to reward strategic behavior. Accordingly, when the next bonuses were allocated, he made a point of ensuring that one of the higher allotments went to an SBU manager who had admirably executed a strategy, not of growth, but of exiting that business. Why? Quite simply because that had been the strategy decided upon, so the manager's performance should be measured against that standard.

This little anecdote underscores an important point: when we measure, we tend to measure behavior and performance. In many ways, this is right and understandable, for we need more than just lip service to the norms and practices of the strategic planning culture: we need results. However, in truth, this should be yet another example of both/and: our aim should be to change both the culture and the performance of the organization. The two objectives should be interlinked and related to one another.

However, this is no easy task. Jack Welch, in his message to shareowners in GE's 1991 Annual Report, highlighted both the extent of this problem and the importance of resolving it:

> Over the past several years we've wrestled at all levels of this company with the question of what we are and what we want to be . . . . we've agreed upon a set of values we believe we will need to take this company forward rapidly through the 1990s and beyond.
>
> In our view, leaders . . . can be characterized in at least four ways.
>
> The first is one who delivers on commitments—financial or otherwise—and shares the values of our company. His or her future is an easy call. Onward and upward.
>
> The second type of leader is one who does not meet commitments and does not share our values. Not as pleasant a call, but equally easy.
>
> The third is one who misses commitments but shares the values. He or she usually gets a second chance, preferably in a different environment.
>
> Then there's the fourth type—the most difficult for many of us to deal with. That leader delivers on commitment, makes all the numbers, but doesn't share the values we must have . . . . the autocrat, the big shot, the

tyrant. Too often all of us have looked the other way—tolerated these "Type 4" managers because "they always deliver"—at least in the short term.

If, therefore, we want to develop a strategic culture, it is clear that we must identify, and reward, type 1 leaders—those who will embody, in thought and action, the principles, values, and practices of the new culture we seek to instill in the organization. For, make no mistake about it, it takes leaders to change a culture.

NOTES

1. Mike Freedman, "Building a Culture for Strategy," in *Strategic Direction* 16, no. 2.

2. From a personal letter, dated 22 March 1984, from Jack Welch to the author.

3. John P. Kotter, and James L. Heskett, *Corporate Culture and Performance* (New York: Free Press, 1992).

4. Peter M. Senge, *The Fifth Discipline: The Art and Practice of the Learning Organization* (New York: Currency Doubleday, 1990).

5. Mark D. Youngblood, "Winning Cultures for the New Economy," *Strategy & Leadership* (November/December 2000): 4–9.

6. Simon London, "Diversity's Big Drawback," *Financial Times,* 25 January 2002.

7. Stephen Shepard, interview, *Business Week,* 28 January 2002.

8. "SAP America Faces up to Challenge of Change," *Financial Times,* 13 June 2001.

9. Youngblood, "Winning Cultures for the New Economy."

10. Donald N. Michael, *On Learning to Plan and Planning to Learn* (San Francisco: Jossey-Bass Publishers, 1973).

11. See the many references to planning sessions mentioned in *Jack: Straight from the Gut.*

12. Edgar H. Schein, *The Corporate Culture Survival Guide* (San Francisco: Jossey-Bass Publishers, 1999).

13. Ralph Waldo Emerson, "Letters and Social Aims."

14. Jack Welch, with John A. Byrne, *Jack: Straight from the Gut* (New York: Warner Business Books), 397.

Chapter 8

THE USE—AND ABUSE—OF METHODOLOGIES

"It is common sense to take a method and try it. If it fails, admit it
frankly and try another. But, above all, try something."
Franklin Delano Roosevelt, address at Oglethorpe University,
Atlanta, Georgia
May 29, 1932

My debunking of what might be termed the "faddishness of methodology" should not be interpreted as a blanket condemnation of methodology as unhelpful and even distracting. If one were cynical, it would be
easy to conclude that the emphasis on a silver bullet methodology has
risen and fallen in direct proportion to the number of academics and
consultants active in the field. However, despite the many false starts
and exaggerated claims, the very proliferation of these tools has been a
good indicator that a market exists for them[1] and that strategic planning
is alive and active in the corporate boardroom.

Clearly, I do not believe that we should dispense with methodology
and rely entirely on intuition and entrepreneurial hunch. As Franklin
Delano Roosevelt observed, it is common sense to experiment with methods, trying them out to see which work and which do not. Our thinking
needs to be disciplined, bounded by logic and reality. And, in this regard,
methodical approaches to planning are clearly helpful and important.

However, two caveats are in order. First, methodologies must not be
allowed to dominate the process as they did in the early days of strategic

planning. Second, companies should introduce new methodologies judiciously, resisting the lure of sheer novelty. Every management system has its own culture when it is working well, there is a delicate balance between tradition and innovation. The introduction of a new methodology inevitably disturbs both the culture and this balance, so decision makers should carefully evaluate the costs as well as the presumed benefits of new tools before they commit to adopting them.

My experience in this field (corroborated by the results of my survey, see Appendix A) indicates that those companies that have progressed furthest in this field do not rely on a single methodology for the effectiveness of their strategic planning and management systems. Best practices suggest that appropriate selectivity is the best guideline here. Both the diversity of business situations and the variety of corporate cultures demand that companies adopt planning tools, techniques, and methodologies that suit their specific situations and requirements rather than relying on a one size fits all approach.

One criterion that I have found useful in determining which methodologies to adopt is their relevance and contribution to the development of a strategic culture in the organization. As I show in chapter 7, at least seven key traits make up a strategic culture, and it makes sense, therefore, that the methodologies we adopt should encourage and reinforce the long-term development of these traits as well as, of course, contribute to the development of specific strategies in the short term.

To illustrate what I have in mind, let us examine a representative collection of eight methodologies to see how they can be woven together to develop the traits we should seek in a strategic culture (see Figure 8.1).

SCENARIO PLANNING

Scenario planning is a strategic management tool to assist executives in their planning and decision making in conditions of uncertainty. Scenarios bound the envelope of uncertainty that confronts decision makers by depicting, in a logical and structured manner, a set of plausible alternative futures with which a company may have to deal. Using scenarios, decision makers can focus on those uncertainties that cannot be eliminated and better assess the risks and payoff of alternative strategy and resource allocation options. (See chapter 6 and Appendix D for further details on scenario planning.)

There are several different approaches to scenario building, but the one referred to in chapter 6 and employed in the case study described

Figure 8.1
Links between Methodologies and Strategic Culture Traits

Methodology	Dealing with Uncertainty	Learning	Organizational Flexibility	Vision	Strategy as Choice	External Focus	"Stretch Goals" (Transformation)
Scenario planning	X	X	X	X	X	X	
Contingency planning	X		X		X	X	
Vulnerability Analysis	X	X		X	X	X	
Benchmarking				X	X	X	X
Options generation	X	X	X	X	X		X
Visioning		X		X	X		X
Business Process Redesign		X	X				X
Total Quality Management	X	X	X			X	X

Key: X = Potential for the methodology to contribute to the development of a strategic culture trait in Appendix D is a six-step process applied by a multidisciplinary team in a series of analyses and workshops:[2]

Step 1: Define the decision focus for the project (i.e., What is the decision to be made at the conclusion of the scenarios?)

Step 2: Identify the key decision factors (i.e., What are the key elements of the future that we would like to know in order to improve the quality of our decision?)

Step 3: Identify and assess the key external forces (i.e., those that will affect the future of the key decision factors)

Step 4: Establish the scenario logics (Scenario logics are the critical axes of uncertainty among these external forces and the organizing principles around which the scenarios are developed)

Step 5: Select and elaborate the scenarios arising from these logics

Step 6: Determine and assess the decision implications of the scenarios (i.e., What are the strategic implications of the scenarios for the decision at hand? What impacts will the scenarios have on the key decision factors?)

The hallmark features of this methodology are the following:

- Decision focus—that is, the starting (and ending) point for the process is the strategic decision the scenarios are designed to address
- Comprehensive analysis of the full range of macroenvironmental and microenvironmental forces affecting the decision
- Scenarios constructed around a set of logics that encompass the critical drivers and uncertainties among these forces
- Elaboration of the scenarios in sufficient detail to identify implications for the decision and to help develop and assess strategy options

Scenario planning can be used both to assist in a single decision and as an integral element in an ongoing strategic planning system. Specifically, it can be applied in the following:

Focused studies in which scenarios are used to assess the evolution of a particular market or technology, identify new applications/uses of a product, or make a key investment decision

Strategic overviews in which scenarios are used as an environmental framework for the strategic thinking of senior management in setting corporate direction and future strategy

Exploratory studies that provide a broad look at the future of, say, the consumer market to assess potential new product and service opportunities

Scenarios thus are closely linked to the development of a number of attributes of a strategic culture. Most obviously, they increase an organization's willingness and ability to deal with uncertainty, to focus on external drivers of the business, and to increase learning and flexibility. But they also contribute to the clarity and farsightedness of vision and to developing strategy as a matter of choice (because of their emphasis on dealing with alternative possibilities in the future).

Scenario planning helps executives deal more effectively with the inherent risks and uncertainties of a rapidly changing business environment. Specifically, scenario planning contributes to the overall effectiveness of strategic management by developing

- A more complete understanding of the dynamics of change
- Fuller consideration of the range of opportunities and threats in the future
- Reduced (not eliminated) vulnerability to surprises
- Expanded range of strategy options
- A more resilient, flexible strategy
- Better assessment of risks

CONTINGENCY PLANNING

Contingency planning is closely linked to scenario planning in their common acknowledgment of the uncertainty of the future and in their shared commitment to being prepared to meet the future, whatever it may bring. In this context we can define contingency as a deviation from one or more of the assumptions on which current corporate strategy is based. Contingency planning is, therefore, concerned with developing a level of corporate preparedness to deal with such deviations, should they occur.

Typically, the steps in this methodology are as follows:

- *Select the major contingencies.* While scenario planning should help in building a degree of resilience into the strategy eventually selected, there will always be contingencies (as defined above) that the strategy does not fully (if at all) address. A review of the scenarios will reveal the range of such contingencies; and, from this range, the management team can select the major ones for which some level of planning should be undertaken.

- *Assign responsibility for monitoring and planning.* To ensure the highest possible level of preparation, the management team should select the individuals or components who are best qualified to monitor and evaluate events related to the development of a contingency and to prepare the necessary plans to deal with it.

- *Identify precursor events.* A key step in the contingency planning process is identifying the precursors of a contingency. By precursor, we mean a trend, event, or development that foreshadows the occurrence of a contingency—that is, it indicates an increase in its probability. It is the establishment of such an early warning system that is key to increasing the ability of an organization to respond, quickly and effectively, should a contingency occur.

- *Develop contingency plans.* Preparedness is dependent on having in place plans that can be put into action as soon as it becomes clear that the contingency has occurred or is about to. Because the plans have to be developed before all the facts are known, it is usually advisable to prepare options for action (e.g., a preferred action and, if all else fails, and alternative action). An important element in this planning is the identification of trigger points—that is, "the point in the development of a contingency at which these plans should be put into action."

- *Monitor events.* The individual or component with assigned responsibility for preparing the contingency plans must also track in detail the actual evolution of events to determine whether the contingency is becoming more or less probable and, in particular, to be alert to the occurrence of trigger points for action.

- *Implement plans.* Should the trigger point occur, the previously prepared plans can then be put into action.

The impact of contingency planning on strategic culture is, like the impact of scenarios, primarily focused on helping an organization to

- Focus clearly on the external forces that shape its future
- Deal constructively (not just defensively) with uncertainty
- Learn its way into the future
- Increase the speed and flexibility of its response to new developments

It also contributes to broadening the scope of strategy as choice through expanding the range of what might be termed contingent strategies, targeted at specific, but uncertain, developments.

VULNERABILITY ANALYSIS

Vulnerability analysis (VA) is an analytical tool developed to uncover the buried knowledge that members of an organization hold about threats and opportunities the company might otherwise overlook. It was originally developed in response to analyses showing that companies' failure to prepare for surprises springs not from a lack of prior information, but from an inability to capture and apply that information. Subsequently, in an effort to develop the entrepreneurial and the defensive elements of an organization, VA evolved to include the identification and assessment of potential opportunities, as well as threats, that may result from developments in the company's business environment.

The VA process usually proceeds in a series of five steps:

- *Preparation.* Determining the true reason(s) for the exercise, reviewing similar work and strategic documents, and selecting and interviewing workshop candidates.

- *Identification of the underpinnings of the business(as distinguished from success factors.* Underpinnings are elements on which the company, and its competitors, depend for their existence, for example, availability of key resources or stability of regulatory climate. This is usually a brainstorming exercise focused on identifying underpinnings in a range of categories (e.g., needs and wants served by the business, resources and assets, customer base, and technologies).

- *Identification of threats and opportunities.* For each underpinning, identifying as many events/forces/conditions as possible that could affect the underpinning (without, at this stage, making any judgment about probability); then, for each event, identifying the threats and opportunities the event might pose. (To avoid overloading a workshop, it is often advisable to hold separate exercises for opportunities and threats.)

- *Evaluation.* Obtaining individual judgments as to likelihood and impact of the events, pooling individual evaluations, interpreting patterns, and establishing priorities for action.

- *Follow-up.* Determining response to VA results and reevaluating and reviewing the results.

VA can be most effectively used as an integral element in strategic planning, at either the corporate or business unit level, both to identify and assess strategic issues and to generate options. It has also been adapted to functional areas such as finance, marketing, and manufacturing. Other applications of this methodology include

- Industry analysis. Assessing the vulnerability of an industry as a whole, with participants from the industry's constituent companies

- Acquisition analysis—Going beyond forecasts of market growth and profitability to examine high-probability/high-impact changes that might threaten the new business

VA is a simple, inexpensive, and effective diagnostic tool that can

- Capture, evaluate, and apply the hidden ideas that are buried in an organization
- Foster awareness of strategic thinking
- Shed light on differences in people's planning assumptions
- Help establish strategic priorities
- Train people to become more alert to emerging opportunities and threats
- Improve communications and relationships between functions and disciplines (through the use of multifunctional workshop teams)

Like scenarios, VA works best through the use of multidisciplinary, multifunctional teams, and thus contributes to the breaking down of internal barriers and an increase in the sharing of information and so to the development of a learning culture. By forcing executives to confront uncertainties (even if they are opportunities rather than threats), it can also do much to increase their ability to deal with uncertainty, their flexibility of thinking and action, and the breadth of their vision.

COMPETITIVE PERFORMANCE PROFILING/ BENCHMARKING

Profiling is a methodology for presenting clear, concise, schematic representations of a the strengths and weaknesses of a company and its competitors. It provides, at a glance, a comprehensive view of the strategic shape of a company and its competitors in a specific industry. In some respects, profiling can be equated with benchmarking, and the comparison can be either against competitors or against world class processes or products in noncompeting companies.

One approach to this profiling, developed while I was at SRI International, can be summarized as follows:[3]

- Identify the four competitive strengths in the industry. Limiting the number focuses attention on the major forces shaping the industry (e.g., technology, marketing, manufacturing, finance)
- Choose one clear, concise measure of success or excellence for each of the four key strengths (e.g., R&D investment, sales, scale, ROI)
- Define the linkages between pairs of competitive strengths (e.g., price as the link between marketing and technology, quality as the link between R&D and manufacturing)
- Define average performance for the industry (with respect to the key strengths and linkages) to use as a yardstick (or benchmark) when assessing competitors' positions

- Generate profiles for the company and key competitors by assessing for each its performance with respect to key strengths and linkages

Profiling is most directly applicable in competitive analysis and competitive strategy development through its focus on key competitive strengths in the industry. By graphically portraying a company's current position relative to its competitors, it helps to identify the areas of needed strategic action and to portray the desired shape (vision) of the company. And, by comparing a company with world class standards (whether or not they are set by direct competitors), it tends to push the company toward the stretch goals needed to achieve superior performance.

This form of profiling is convenient, easy to apply, and requires no special skills. It leverages to the full the benefits of displaying assessments graphically in order to

- Condense and apply, quickly and easily, management's understanding of the industry and their own competitive position
- Focus attention on key drivers and success factors
- Reach consensus on competitive and needed company actions to achieve competitive advantage

OPTIONS GENERATION AND EVALUATION

Since one of the key principles of a strategic culture is that strategy should be a matter of choice, some methodology aimed at generating and evaluating strategy options is key to providing executives with an effective range of genuine options. Whatever methodology is chosen, it should be designed to provide a structured approach to developing options that are

- Distinct, not just slight variations of a base case
- Plausible, that is, they are truly consistent with external realities and internal capabilities
- Well developed, with sufficient rationale and detail to provide a sound basis for executive decision making

The essence of this methodology is a structured six-step approach and the use of measures to stimulate individual and group creativity:

1. *Establishing guidelines*—assumptions about the macro- and micro-environment; statements of strategic objectives; criteria for evaluating alternatives

2. *Preparation.* Clarifying strategic issues, analyzing uncontrollables that may limit or define options, and reviewing methods for enhancing group creativity

3. *Developing decision categories.* That is, variables to be considered in developing options (e.g., product range, markets to be served, resource commitments, alliances)

4. *Creating alternatives.* Options for each decision category; brainstorming without evaluation

5. *Synthesis.* Combining options for each decision category into a comprehensive, logical, internally consistent strategy

6. *Packaging the results.* Summarizing results of the options exercise, with rationale, pros and cons, resource requirements, and risks and rewards for each option

Options generation and assessment comes into play at the heart of the strategy development process (see Figure 3.1). It can draw on the product of many other methodologies—strategic mapping, scenarios, and value chain analysis, for example—as sources of creative ideas for options. And it links up with other methodologies—analytic hierarchy process, for example[4]—to evaluate the relative attractiveness and resilience of the options generated.

In terms of its impact on strategic culture, options generation is clearly central to the notion of strategy as choice and a major contributor to the development of strategic vision. In addition, an organization's flexibility and ability to deal with uncertainty is dependent on having a range of truly different courses of action to chose from.

The key benefit from generating options before making a strategic decision is that the resulting strategy is more likely to be the most imaginative, competitive, and profitable option available. Without options, planning by default (continuing to follow familiar paths) or adopting a strategy that satisfices (barely meets the minimum conditions) is unlikely to meet the demands of a changing and uncertain environment.

- Deciding without options usually means that management will continue to follow established paths even at a time when a change of course is needed.

- Choice among options provides the opportunity to select from significantly different strategic directions.

- Generating alternatives at an early stage of planning helps focus strategy development on the trade-offs that may be required.

- Creating alternatives forces executives and staff to design solutions to strategic issues as integral elements in an overall business strategy.
- Creating options enlarges the horizon and vision of strategic thinking.

VISIONING

Strategic vision is a coherent and powerful statement of what the organization can and should be (ten) years hence (the time horizon varies with the nature of the business). It defines key elements of the desired future corporation—its scope, scale, competitive focus, product/market focus, image and relationships, and organization and culture—and is used to generate commitment and motivate performance in implementing the strategy. (See chapter 5 for further details on strategic vision.)

Developing a strategic vision for a company is an integral part of the strategy development process and follows many of the same steps employed in that process, namely, the following:

- Identify potential opportunities and threats to answer the question, "What are we allowed or forced to be?"
- Assess the company's strengths and weaknesses, to answer the question, "Realistically, what can we be?"
- Clarify management values, to answer the question, "What do we want to be?"
- Develop (or revise) a mission statement
- Identify strategic objectives and goals
- Generate, assess, and select strategic options
- Develop the vision statement
- Conduct sanity checks to test the vision against reality

The two central applications of strategic vision are, first, to integrate the discrete elements of strategic analysis into a coherent and consistent whole; and, second, to drive implementation of the strategy by motivating performance. In the process, visioning contributes to the development of a strategic culture, most obviously by making strategy and its execution more visionary and also by encouraging managers to set stretch goals. Vision is, thus, an essential element in organizational change, focusing on the need for transformational rather than incremental change.

The power of visioning is demonstrated through its ability to

- Add value to strategic planning
- Convey the totality of the changes the organization must make

- Change the way an organization thinks of itself and operates
- Catalyze, focus, and energize action throughout the organization
- Sustain the drive toward implementation of strategy
- Restore the balance between managing and leading
- Improve performance, and therefore, profitability

BUSINESS PROCESS REDESIGN/ REENGINEERING[5]

Business process redesign (BPR) is an approach to transforming the business process of an organization to achieve breakthroughs in quality, flexibility, responsiveness, and cost. Typically, the process starts with a blank sheet of paper in order to encourage a radical rethinking of existing processes to deliver more value to the customer. BPR uses a combination of industrial engineering, operations research, management theory, quality management, and systems analysis in order to (1) redesign business processes and (2) harness the power of information technology to support the restructured processes more effectively. Companies typically adopt a new value system that places increased emphasis on customer needs, reduces organizational layers, and eliminates unproductive activities in two key areas—by redesigning functional organizations into cross-functional teams; and by using technology to improve data dissemination and decision making.

BPR aims at generating radical change initiatives through a five-step process:

1. Refocus company values on customer needs
2. Redesign core processes to maximize speed and flexibility and minimize redundancy and bureaucracy, often using information technology to facilitate improvements
3. Reorganize the business into cross-functional teams with end-to-end responsibility for a process
4. Rethink basic people and organizational issues
5. Improve business processes across the organization

BPR is used to improve performance on key processes that impact customers, with the following objectives:

Reduce the cost and cycle time by eliminating unproductive activities. Reorganizing by teams decreases the need for management layers, accelerates information flows, and eliminates the errors and rework caused by multiple handoffs.

Improve quality by reducing the fragmentation of work and establishing clear ownership of processes.

In terms of culture change, BPR increases a corporation's learning capability by breaking down internal barriers to the sharing of knowledge and so heightens the flexibility and speed of the organization's response to change.

BPR improves the strategic performance of a business by

- Developing a fresh perspective on customer satisfaction
- Taking a process approach to the corporation's business
- Enhancing a company's strength in each of the key areas of strategic vision (see Visioning, pp 117f), not just its competitiveness
- Using information technology appropriately as an enabler of change

TOTAL QUALITY MANAGEMENT

Total quality management (TQM) is a systematic method of economically producing goods, services, and information that meet customers' performance requirements. TQM defines quality in terms of customer satisfaction (rather than the organization's internal standards) and aims to produce products and services to specifications with zero defects. It seeks to extend quality improvement into every aspect of a company's operations.

TQM is more of an approach to managing than a methodology. In broad terms, it requires managers to

Assess customer requirements

- Understand present and future customer needs
- Design products and services that cost-effectively meet—or exceed—those needs

Deliver quality

- Identify the key problem areas in the process and work on them until they approach zero-defect levels
- Train employees to use the new processes
- Develop effective measure of product and service quality
- Create incentives linked to quality goals
- Promote zero-defect philosophy across all activities

- Encourage management to lead by example
- Develop feedback mechanisms to ensure continuous improvement

TQM can be applied to any systematic attempt to restructure strategy, organization, and culture, focusing on a customer orientation and rethinking of current practices. As such, it links up with, and can use the techniques and perspectives of, time to market, business process redesign, and benchmarking.

TQM focuses on improving critical operations using both new and proven methods to achieve the following benefits:

- Better understanding of customer needs
- Designing products and services to meet those needs
- Implementing business systems and processes throughout the organization to produce those products and services while avoiding and preventing problems, with the bottom-line results of increased customer satisfaction, reduced costs, and heightened internal motivation

SOME GUIDELINES ON USING METHODOLOGIES

To sum up, then, methodologies, properly used, are useful and essential elements in strategic planning. The trick is to harness them and not allow them to dominate the process as they did in the 1970s.

There are some rules of thumb that we should bear in mind, particularly when considering the introduction of a new (for us) methodology:

- *Consider carefully the full cost of introducing a new methodology.* The cost includes far more than the expense of education and training programs, consulting fees, and (possibly) the addition of new staff. There are potentially much higher—often hidden—costs associated with the inevitable disruption of established routine, the learning of a new way of doing things, and relearning the revised planning process.

- *Methodology should contribute not just to the development of strategy, but also to the creation or reinforcement of a strategic culture.* It goes without saying that the methodology should make a specific and identifiable contribution to the development of strategy, as Royal Dutch/ Shell did when they adopted scenario planning to deal with the traumatic uncertainties of the 1970s energy scene. Otherwise, why consider it? What may not be so obvious, however, is its contribution to the creation of a strategic culture. In an age when strategy is being defined and redefined virtually constantly, and the life span of a particular strategic thrust is often measured in months rather than years, it is vital that the organization develop a culture that is capable of dealing with such a problem. That is why I put such stress on the importance of linking methodologies to specific strategic culture traits (see Figure 8.1).

- *Make sure that the methodologies are compatible.* Soft methodologies, such as scenarios and visioning, for example, will have a hard time taking root in a climate dominated by hard methodologies such as econometric modeling and discounted cash flow. The two types are not inherently incompatible, but the problems of fit are real and have to be addressed.

- *Beware the next big thing.* Predictably, new methodologies will be developed and touted as the next big thing, as TQM, reengineering, core competences, and share owner value have been in the past, and as market migration analysis and knowledge management are currently. What we need to recognize is that these and other methodologies are not substitutes for strategic planning: they are part of it and must be viewed as such. It is always a mistake to adopt a new methodology indiscriminately without tailoring it to the needs and culture of the organization. But the worst mistake of all would be to junk strategic planning—yet again—in the belief that the new methodology was the magic formula for which we have all along been seeking.

NOTES

1. See Appendix E for two listings of strategic planning methodologies.

2. The scenario methodology described in this volume is essentially that developed by SRI International and Royal Dutch/Shell.

3. For a fuller description of this methodology, see Emilio Cvitkovic, "A Methodology to Analyze Competitors' Skills: Performance Profiles," in *Competition: Forms, Facts and Fiction* (London: The Macmillan Press, Ltd., 1993), 83–90.

4. Analytic Hierarchy Process (AHP) is a mathematical decision analysis methodology used to rank the importance or desirability of a set of activities or criteria. AHP assists decision makers by providing a framework for describing and analyzing the many factors, priorities, and considerations that enter into a relatively complex selection process.

5. Michael Hammer and James Champy, *Reengineering the Corporation: A Manifesto for Business Revolution* (New York: Harper Business, 1994).

Chapter 9

WHAT OF THE FUTURE?

STRATEGY IN THE POST–9/11 WORLD

Inevitably the questions arise, "Isn't strategy largely irrelevant in the turmoil of the post–9/11 world? Aren't we confronted with a whole new ball game? Hasn't uncertainty reached such a level that strategy is impractical and our best response now lies in tactical flexibility?" The questions are reasonable, and the frustration that underlies them is understandable. But Michael Porter's assertion that "the need for strategy has never been greater" is still valid and for the same reason: The greater the number of inflection points and the higher the level of uncertainty that an organization has to deal with, the greater is its need for a sense of purpose, direction, and continuity—in a word, for a strategy.[1]

This is not to say that nothing has changed in the world of strategy as a result of September 11, 2001. Quite obviously, it has, and we can see the changes developing at three levels.

First, and most obvious, is the need to develop what we might call a security strategy—a systematic approach to protecting organizations (particularly corporations) against discontinuities of all sorts, not just those arising from terrorist attacks. As Ralph Shrader and Mike McConnell pointed out in their article, "Security and Strategy in the Age of Discontinuity," the events of 9/11 did not represent a change in the nature of discontinuities (Peter Drucker had foreseen many of them a decade and more ago) so much as an increase in our vulnerability to what they term "interdependence risk—the potential for ostensibly small events. . . . to spiral rapidly into a company-threatening crisis."[2] (James Gleick, in his book on chaos theory, makes a similar point with his observations on the "butterfly effect" in weather forecasting—the fact that relatively small changes can cascade upward rapidly into continent-sized perturbations.[2]) Protecting companies requires, they argue, "the integration of organizational security and corporate strategy," focusing on three primary objectives: (1) Reducing the vulnerability of employees, (2) protecting the critical operations and facilities of the core business, and (3) securing the networks of information systems, knowledge communities, alliances, and links with customers and suppliers with the overall goal of achieving security "in an open environment and within the context of a corporate strategy designed to facilitate growth and profitability."[3]

At the second level, the events of 9/11 and their aftermath have imposed on many companies the need to rethink and reformulate the strategies for their basic businesses. Most particularly, airlines and other travel-related companies, financial services, and insurance, energy, and computer networking industries will have to reexamine key elements in their current strategies and operations, including marketing, globalization, the location and redundancy of facilities, and relations with governments.

At any even broader level, the concept of corporate strategy will have to be expanded and redefined to include a company's actions to deal not just with market and competitive forces, but also with a new array of social and political requirements (see Box 9.1). As I noted in my book, *The New Rules of Corporate Conduct*,[4] this new element of strategy entails much closer working with governments and a more proactive strategy in responding to the challenges that these new requirements present. The objective here is not just to make for an easier passage for a particular company, but rather to ensure the continued acceptance and expansion of the global enterprise system whose currently perceived faults—globalization, materialism, and economic imperialism—are particularly cited as the special targets of Islamic terrorist groups, for instance. *"The next decade,"* I wrote, *"will be a critical testing time for democracy, market systems, and (by extension) the private corporation"* (emphasis in original).

Thirdly, it is safe to say that these events and their aftermath have heightened the importance of some of the values and methodologies that, as I have suggested earlier, are key elements in strategic thinking and action. An outstanding example is the needed strategic response to the

---

Box 9.1
The New Rules of Corporate Conduct

Legitimacy. To earn and retain social legitimacy, the corporation must define its basic mission in terms of the social purpose it is deigned to serve rather than as the maximization of profits.

Governance. The corporation must be thought of, managed, and governed more as a community of stakeholders and less as the property of investors.

Equity. The corporation must strive to achieve greater perceived fairness in the distribution of economic wealth and in its treatment of all stakeholder interests.

Environment. The corporation must integrate the practices of restorative economics and sustainable development into the mainstream of its business strategy.

Employment. The corporation must rewrite the social contract of work to reflect the values of the new work force and increase both the effectiveness and loyalty of employees and the corporation.

Public-private sector relationships. To ensure the success of the power shift, corporations must work closely with governments to achieve a viable and publicly accepted redefinition of the roles and responsibilities of the public and private sectors.

Ethics. The corporation must elevate and monitor the level of ethical performance in all its operations in order to build the trust that is the foundation of sound relationships with all stakeholder groups.

---

dramatic increase in uncertainty, discontinuity, and interdependence risks. These developments have put a premium on the contribution that three methodologies—scenarios, vulnerability analysis, and contingency planning (see chapter 8)—can make to the development of a more resilient strategy. And most surely they underscore the importance of learning, flexibility, vision, and the ability to deal with uncertainty as essential traits in the corporate culture.

A LOOK AHEAD

In the past 30 or so years, strategic planning has, as we have already noted, passed through periods of growth, near-fatal errors, adjustment, and reform. In the next 10 years, we can hope for a period of maturity that will reflect balance, focus, and an emphasis on basics.

Attempts to map out the future course of strategic management more precisely are apt to confuse the predictive with the prescriptive: the observer's views of what ought to happen cloud judgments about what will happen. Nonetheless, the evidence suggests that strategic management is here to stay. Ten years ago, we could not have been so sure. However, corporations have corrected the errors and excesses of their earlier efforts. The process is now more nimble, relevant, and productive. And the need for strategic thinking has never been greater. With economic, political, competitive, and technological restructuring in full gear, some sort of strategic sense must guide executive decision making. The only questions are how companies will develop this sense, what tools they will use, and what priorities they will set.

Humanization of the Process

Lester Thurow, dean of the Sloan School of Management at the Massachusetts Institute of Technology, used to point out one little-noted difference between U.S. and Japanese corporations. In the United States, he noted, the number-two executive in a corporation is usually the chief operating officer or chief financial officer; in Japan, that executive is more likely to be the chief human resources officer. A look at recent developments suggests that more and more corporations, in all Triad countries, will be following Japan's example.

Organizational and cultural problems dominate the list of internal challenges facing strategic management. Increasingly, executives recognize that strategic success depends heavily on the way in which companies pursue the development of managers, the motivation of employees, the flexibility of the structure, and the free flow of communications. Speed, simplicity, and self-confidence are the organizational and individual qualities that Jack Welch promoted when he spoke of "soft values for a hard decade." Empowerment, business process redesign, and team building are the tools that strategic management now emphasizes to secure competitive advantage.

These facts mean that human resource strategy will play a greater role in overall business strategy. Having largely closed the gap between planning and operations, companies now find that a deeper and harder challenge is to create a culture that makes implementation possible. Thus, we can expect human resource managers to have a greater say in the design of management processes and in the development of strategy. An early sign of this trend was the appointment, in 1992, of Frank Doyle as a member of GE's top triumvirate (along with Welch and Paolo Fresco), following a career in human resources. Ten years from now, such a background may still be an exception at the top, but the direction remains clear.

The Systemization of Strategic Intelligence

Improved understanding of the changing business environment is one of the top three benefits of strategic management that respondents cited in my survey. Not surprisingly, therefore, many companies have started to upgrade their environmental analysis efforts. But major gaps remain. In my consulting, I have noted that many companies lack critical information about even such traditional business areas as markets, competition, and technology. In many cases, the problem is not so much a failure to gather information as an absence of systematic collation and interpretation. How many times has a company discovered, after the fact, that it did possess the intelligence forewarning of a critical shift in its markets or competition but underestimated or failed to understand its significance or did not bring this information to the attention of decision makers? Monsanto, for instance, had warnings from its European staff that genetically modified foods would not enjoy the easy market and regulatory acceptance that they had in the United States. The trouble was their warnings were not loud enough.

The most obvious area for expansion lies in the collection, analysis, and retrieval of strategic intelligence. Noting the increased role that executives play in environmental analysis, Ian Morrison, one-time president of the Institute for the Future, noted that "one clear implication of this shift . . . is that executives need new tools to gather, distill, synthesize, analyze, and reflect on the wide range of complex environmental information." The old strategic planning process was good at gathering vast amounts of strategic intelligence in one central spot. The challenge for the new strategic management process is to emulate the old process but in a more decentralized and efficient fashion. We have a major opportunity to expand the use of information management, particularly in view of the likely systemization of strategic intelligence systems.

A more problematic area is direct use of the personal computer in strategy development. As far back as 1993, *Planning Review* reported, in its March/April issue, on the success of an ambitious knowledge-based software system that runs on PCs and aims to help planners develop strategic plans. Using responses to 400 questions, the program was able to generate a coherent strategic plan that included observations about the business, key factors influencing the success of the business, strengths and weaknesses of the company, and predictions for the success of different strategic options. The planners who participated in this experiment were impressed by the program's ability to provide new insights in some areas and appreciated its ability to provide a logic trail for all its conclusions. However, they identified some drawbacks, noting in particular the inability of the program to incorporate some complexities unique to their business.

Several factors will inherently limit the application of PC programs in the more creative phases of strategy development (such as scenarios development, options generation, and creation of a strategic vision). For instance, knowledge-based programs (and the algorithms underlying them) are inherently past oriented: they rely on lessons from past experience and so may be of limited help (and even inappropriate) in radically new conditions. Further, managers now consider strategic thinking a fundamental requirement for a successful process, and anything that seems to short-circuit or downplay executive thinking will have a hard time gaining acceptance. Finally, manipulation of computer programs is typically a staff function rather than an executive one, and increased use of these programs is apt, therefore. to lead back to one of the seven deadly sins—namely, the imposition of staff work on what should be an executive function. Indeed, with some justification, the typical executive reaction might be summed up with the retort, "The PC chose the strategy: let the PC implement it!"

However, there are many information-rich phases in the strategy development process, including environmental monitoring and scanning, options assessment, implementation planning, and measurement of results. And here there are many opportunities for harnessing the PC as a valuable strategic-planning tool.

The Demise of the Planning Calendar

The notion of a fixed calendar for the planning cycle is deeply rooted in corporate mythology. "We strategize in the spring and plan in the fall," Robert Pry, then strategic planner for Gould Inc., once mused. Now the move away from a fixed planning calendar—an undeviating annual sequence of strategy, operational plans, and budgets—has already begun. People have long been aware that this rhythm is too slow for many businesses and unnecessarily rapid for the few that are fortunate enough to enjoy a measure of market stability. Some companies have, therefore, tailored their planning calendars to the varying business situations of their SBUs. On this score alone, the planning calendar is out of sync with the tempo of the times: it is a holdover from the days when schedules—and the environment—were more predictable.

The more serious defect of this annual cycle, however, is that it is at odds with one of the basic precepts of strategic management (as opposed to planning)—namely, that it is a continuing process in which planning and operations overlap rather than occur sequentially. Therefore, building a management schedule around a planning cycle makes little sense, particularly around a cycle that entails a complete iteration of all the planning steps (situation assessment, issues identification, options generation, and so on), regardless of whether or not the situation requires it.

In the next few years, the movement away from the fixed planning calendar will, in all probability, accelerate. Though short-term operations planning and budgeting will continue to be annual tasks (a) relic of our agricultural past with its emphasis on the annual cycle of weather), the strategic planning and thinking elements of management will more and more depart from set schedules and become an ongoing part of running the business.

The End of the Methodologies Lock

In the early days of strategic planning, methodology and procedure were virtually everything. They had a lock on the process, on the staff who used them, and on the executives they were supposed to help. This unhealthy situation has been changing and seems likely to disappear in the next 10 years.

One can make the case that we already have all the methodologies that we require and that the next step is to learn to use the right mix of existing methodologies. Certainly, a point of diminishing returns is approaching, with methodologies and processes offering only minor differences from one another. In the recent past, corporate executives have been called upon to try and distinguish between core competences and core capabilities, between the virtual corporation and the modular corporation, and between the learning organization and high-performance teams. Overlap and redundancy have been extreme.

That situation cannot be allowed to continue. Executives and planners have become more sophisticated purchasers and users of new methodologies, skeptical of claimed benefits, and rightly aware of the culture shock that any new approach entails. As a result, methodology will return to its place as means rather than end, and its lock on process and thinking will have been broken.

SO WHAT SHOULD WE DO NOW?

There are, I believe, two key lessons that the erratic course strategic planning has followed over the past 30 years should have taught us. One is the futility of relying on any one methodology as the silver bullet that will ensure strategic success. Second, if we are to get the best results from our efforts at strategic planning, we must recognize that it requires a sustained commitment, an understanding of its subtlety and complexity, and a harnessing of strategic opposites. This final point has been articulated in various ways by a variety of authors. Richard Pascale has written a book on "how the smartest companies use conflict to stay ahead."[5] Thomas Stewart has described "nine dilemmas leaders face," and Percy Barnevik, former CEO of ABB Brown Boveri, made a positive virtue out of three contradictions in the company's strategy:[6]

> We want to be global and local, big and small, radically decentralized with centralized reporting and control. If we resolve these contradictions, we create organizational advantage.

If strategic planning is to continue to make the contribution to corporate success that it can, we need to move further and faster toward a holistic, both/and approach to these (and other) interlinked elements of strategy. It is not, as I have pointed out, a matter of balancing these opposites, for balancing suggests an equilibrium, a middle-of-the-road strategy, and an equal pursuit of these two poles. Harnessing the power of opposites better conveys the idea I have in mind. We examine each pole in turn to determine what power it can bring to bear on the strategic issues we face and then harness that power to help drive the overall business strategy.

The question then arises: What should we do if we are to get the full benefit of strategic planning? There are at least four cautionary messages that this examination of its past erratic history convey to us.

1. *Strategic planning is not a sometime thing: it cannot be turned on and off like a faucet and still be effective.* Strategy requires a long-term commitment. The on again/off again approach of the past 20 years clearly has to stop. This is not to say that the process should be frozen for all time and that no improvement in methodology should be allowed (although an argument can be made that we have all the methodology we need, if we would but use it effectively!). However, we need to make a long-term commitment to strategic planning and stabilize the situation so that no longer will *Business Week* feel compelled to report yet another death (or rebirth) of strategic planning.

2. *Any strategy that aims to be sustainable over the long haul requires the harnessing of opposite forces.* Attention to one force while ne-

glecting the opposite will, inevitably, lead to a deficiency and, ultimately disruption, in the organization's performance.

3. *Focus less on process and more on the creative thinking, the strategic capability that it should generate.* To this extent, Mintzberg was right: most managers are overly enamored of neatness in their processes, looking for strategy by the numbers. But the creative process that is at the heart of good strategy development is not that neat. Welch referred to it as "wallowing" around in ideas. What we need is a process that is sufficiently tight to give structure to our thinking but sufficiently loose to give fullest expression to our intuition and imagination.

4. Finally, there is the point that I stressed in the chapter 8: *Beware the next big thing.*

SOME FINAL THOUGHTS

Strategy is a subtle art because it has no option but to deal with uncertainty. No longer does it have the luxury of relying on firm projections of the future or of developing fixed plans that can be executed without change or question. Rather, it must, at one and the same time, be both flexible enough to respond to sudden changes and definitive enough to make a difference—for vacillating is a prescription for losing in these competitive times.

It is a subtle art, too, because it has to harness the power of opposites, of sometimes seemingly conflicting considerations, in determining its future course. It cannot, for instance, succeed for long by serving the short term at the expense of the long term, and it cannot reach the long term if it neglects the immediate needs of the present. Nor is there any algorithm that will provide an easy solution, with mathematical precision, to this problem. The answer will come only from the exercise of executive judgment, with all its failings and limitations.

Strategy is a subtle art because it must be visionary without being impractical. The vision must be specific and inspiring enough to become the driving force of the organization yet allow great latitude in the tactics for getting there. It is often the product of an inspiring leader; but it is nothing if it does not become a shared vision.

Strategy is a subtle art because it depends far more on the power of creative thinking than on any formulaic approach. Methodologies are a necessary tool: they can be used to highlight issues, evaluate options, project outcomes, allocate resources, and provide a framework for our thinking. But they cannot supply the creative spark that generates the winning strategy. It can come only from the interplay of creative minds and the drive of focused action.

Strategy is a subtle art because it requires a supportive culture, and culture is notoriously difficult and elusive to develop. As we have already noted, so many factors—organizational inertia, comfort level with the familiar, managerial resistance, and vested interests in the status quo— are arrayed against culture change that only a forceful and persuasive leader can effect the change and then only with difficulty and over time.

But nowhere is the subtlety and difficulty of strategy more apparent than in the fact that so few corporate strategies enjoy lasting success. Today's success stories seem, with few exceptions, to become tomorrow's failures. And failure can come from many sources—a failure of vision, a failure of perception, a failure of resolve, a failure of flexibility, and even a failure in execution.[7] So perhaps the final lesson that experience should teach us is that Don Michael was right: if we are going to learn to plan, we must plan to learn, and learn constantly and comprehensively. We must learn from our customers, learn from our competitors, learn from the signals of change in our environment, and (above all) learn from our own mistakes.

NOTES

1. Michael E. Porter, "Corporate Strategy: The State of Strategic Thinking," *The Economist*, 23 May 1987, 17–22.

2. Ralph W. Shrader and Mike McConnell, "Security and Strategy in the Age of Discontinuity," *Strategy + Business* (first quarter 2002).

3. James Gleick, *Chaos: Making of a New Science* (New York: Viking Penguin, Inc., 1987).

4. Ian Wilson, *The New Rules of Corporate Conduct: Rewriting the Social Charter* (Westport, Conn.: Quorum Books, 2000).

5. Richard Tanner Pascale, *Managing on the Edge: How the Smartest Companies Use Conflict to Stay Ahead* (New York: Touchstone, Simon & Schuster, 1990).

6. Interview with Percy Barnevik in *Harvard Business Review* (March/April 1991).

7. A recent book, *Execution: The Discipline of Getting Things Done* (New York: Crown Business/Random House, 2002), addresses this last problem. The authors, Larry Bossidy (former vice chairman of GE, and CEO of Honeywell) and Ram Charan (consultant and educator) argue that the biggest problem that organizations face is the inability to turn goals into reality—what they call "execution."

Appendix A

SURVEY OF STRATEGIC
MANAGEMENT PRACTICES

Clearly, strategic planning practices have been changing in recent years. In an effort to gain some perspective on the degree and direction of these changes, I conducted a survey of nearly 50 corporations about their current practices and the changes that had recently occurred in their organizations. Although the survey is clearly not a statistically accurate sample, respondents represented a wide variety of industries, including resources (oil and gas, paper, and aluminum), chemicals, pharmaceuticals, machine tools, office equipment, electronics, utilities (electricity, gas, and telecommunications), and defense. Responding companies were predominantly from the Triad regions—15 in North America (the United States and Canada), 12 in Europe (Belgium, Finland, Germany, Italy, the Netherlands, Norway, Spain, and Switzerland), and 17 in Japan. The diversity and stature of the respondents—including such globally known names as Amoco, Ameritech, Du Pont, and General Electric in North America; British Gas, Philips, ENI, and Elf-Aquitaine in Europe; and Matsushita Electric, NEC, and NTT in Japan—make the findings particularly significant.

CHANGES IN EMPHASIS AND APPROACH

The major shifts in strategic management during the 1980s were toward increasing emphasis on the externalities of the business and changing the locus of planning responsibility within the corporation. These shifts are clearly corporate responses to the criticisms that brought the early models of strategic planning into such disrepute a decade earlier. The planning models of the 1970s tended to be overly concerned with the manipulation of internal financial data, and they were largely staff driven.

Japanese survey respondents differed from their North American and European counterparts by reporting more change in their emphasis on core competences and technology strategy and less change in their emphasis on competitive and market analyses and in redefining the roles of managers and staff. One interpretation of this difference is that Japanese companies were already well advanced in their market orientation and so have devoted relatively more attention to core competences and technology strategy that were more recent arrivals on the strategic planning scene.

Heightening the External Emphasis

Not surprisingly, in view of the radical industry and market restructuring of recent years, more sophisticated attention to changing market and competitive conditions—and to identifying and strengthening core competences to deal with these conditions—has become key to successful strategic positioning. The majority of respondents indicated that the greatest change in their planning systems has occurred in these two prime areas. In most cases, change has been more in the company culture than in the level of analysis and monitoring.

Executives have clearly heeded the advice of both Tom Peters ("Stay close to your customer") and Michael Porter ("Rethink competitive positioning") in redefining the primary tasks of strategic planning. And this book learning has had strong, sometimes brutal, reinforcement from the lessons executives have had to learn from a business environment that is changing rapidly under the hammer blows of globalized competition, new technology, economic uncertainties, rapid shifts in government regulations, and the new demographics of consumer markets. Indeed, many of the methodologies that companies have adopted (see the section "The Use of New Methodologies" in this appendix) and respondents' conviction that "improved understanding of the changing business environment" is one of the prime benefits of strategic planning reflect this new emphasis in strategic planning. This new emphasis is far more than a change in strategic planning methodology. Corporations are recognizing that they must change their thinking and behavior—the very essence of corporate culture—to deal with a new environment and to become truly what they always said they were: market oriented.

All the more surprising, therefore, is that corporations have done so little to expand their efforts in contingency planning, even though they acknowledge the inherent uncertainty of external forces. Only one-quarter of the respondents said they had put more effort into contingency planning, and no one can make a convincing case that they had already developed efforts in this area so well that little or no change was necessary. The frequency of shocks and surprises in virtually every industry during the 1980s has evidently increased decision makers' use of scenario planning but has done little to change their ingrained tendency to rely on a go-for-broke approach to strategy.

Changing the Internal Locus of Planning Responsibility

The survey confirms what observers have long suspected: Responsibility for strategic management has shifted from staff to line managers and from the corporate level to the SBU level. Both moves have been aimed at dealing with the problem that nearly sank strategic planning: the lack of implementation.

The source of this problem is to be found in the way strategic planning originated in the early 1970s. As with most new organizational approaches, strategic planning had its introduction at the corporate level and became the responsibility of a new staff component. And like most staff components in those days, this one rapidly took on the trappings of bureaucracy. Staff multiplied (by 1980, GE had nearly 200 senior level planners on the payroll, at corporate and SBU levels); procedures became standardized (so that they could be taught, and results compared across SBUs); methodologies proliferated; and the plan became an end in itself. Not surprisingly, in the process, strategic thinking short-circuited, and executives' roles were virtually reduced to rubber-stamping staff recommendations. The evidence of this survey is, therefore, an encouraging indication that responsibility is moving from staff to line managers, where it should have resided in the first place.

Although the survey is ambivalent about the role of documentation—nearly equal numbers of respondents say that either major or little or no change has occurred in their documentation processes—my own anecdotal experience indicates that the bulk and formality of planning documents have decreased and no longer dominate the planning process. Although few companies have gone as far as Jack Welch in stripping away the overlay of planning volumes, most companies now place much greater emphasis on the thinking behind the words and on focused executive dialogue about the critical issues facing the business.

THE CHALLENGES TO STRATEGIC MANAGEMENT

Having evolved from its purely planning focus, strategic management faces both external and internal challenges with which it must grapple and internal barriers to its successful execution. This survey elicited few surprises regarding the external challenges that respondents cited but generated some surprising assertions about the internal problems.

External Challenges

When one analyzes the responses to the question in Table A.1, the reasoning behind the increased external emphasis in strategic management is immediately

Table A.1
The Challenges to Strategic Management

What, in your opinion, are the three most critical external -- and internal -- challenges to successful strategic management in your company?

External Challenges (Number of mentions)	Internal Challenges (Number of mentions)
Political change and government policies (17)	Corporate culture (38)
Economic forces/restructuring (18)	Management skills, commitment (19)
Technological change (12)	Strategic planning process (11)
Competition (18)	Financial challenges (18)
Market shifts (21)	Operational problems (15)
Environmental factors (8)	Innovation (16)
Other social forces (7)	

apparent. The tumultuous uncertainty of social, economic, political, and technological forces has virtually changed the rules of the game for many industries, and companies' planning efforts have had to adapt to these changes. Collectively, the impacts of this multifold restructuring dominate corporate thinking, and the evidence that respondents cite to support their statements covers a wide, but largely predictable, range of specifics. Perhaps the only surprising finding—surprising, that is, when one considers the now common corporate mantra that we are now in the 'age of the environment'—is the relatively low emphasis placed on environmental issues. Possibly, however, this change in corporate emphasis has yet to play out.

Political Change and Government Policies

Government policy, regulations, and intervention in the corporate decision-making process have long been traditional corporate anathema that executives viewed with the same inevitability that the public ascribes to death and taxes. This survey, however, revealed a new set of concerns: the degree of uncertainty that corporations say they are encountering on the political scene—uncertainty about the future balance between national and regional interests in trading blocs, uncertainty about the outcome of many countries' experiments with deregulation and market-oriented policies, and uncertainty in the geopolitical arena as Russia and China try to reestablish themselves as powers in the new political order. Indeed, it is the instability and unpredictability of the political scene that companies cite most often as major concerns. As I noted in my book, *The New Rules of Corporate Conduct: Rewriting the Social Charter,* the power shift in the relationship between public and private sectors in many countries can be profoundly unsettling to corporations because it entails, simultaneously, the possibility of relaxed economic regulation, increased competition, and heightened public expectations of corporate performance.

Economic Forces and Restructuring

In addition to citing traditional concerns about the state of the economy, the level of interest rates, and the volatility of foreign exchange rates, respondents cited the challenges of anticipating and dealing with globalization and its accompanying economic and industrial restructuring. In industry after industry, these forces are changing both the number and the type of players and the basic rules of the game. In the process, a clear shift has occurred in the focus, emphasis, and methodology of strategic management to speed corporate adaptation to these changes.

Technological Change

The technological challenge, according to respondents, lies not only in the pace and diversity of change itself, but also in the scale of corporate response necessary to keep abreast of changes. Nowadays the primary challenge would seem to be developing a new, competitive E-business model for the company that balances the bricks and clicks elements in its approach to markets. Among other challenges, respondents cited institutional resistance to change, the rapidly increasing scale of required investment, and the problems of acquiring and evaluating truly strategic intelligence from the massive data flows of the so-called information explosion.

Competition and Market Shifts

Arising out of political, economic, technological, and social changes, structural shifts on both sides of the market—the changing needs and mix of consumers and the sources, strategies, and intensity of competition—have forced planners and executives alike to devote more meticulous and sophisticated attention to interpreting signals from their markets and their competitors. (As I noted above, this new emphasis manifests itself more in North American and European companies than it does in Japan.)

Environmental Factors

Survey responses give some indication of just how far most companies are from integrating environmental strategy into their overall business planning. Only eight companies cited the environment as a strategic concern, despite a heavy representation of energy, chemical, and automobile industries in the sample, and in most cases the issue was predominantly added costs rather than a challenge to develop a proactive strategy to secure competitive advantage.

Other Social Factors

The items mentioned in this category are a small reflection of the growing impact of social pressures on corporate performance. Urban crime and litigiousness, increasing public expectations of corporate performance, relationships with multiple stakeholders, and the problems of dealing with other cultures in a globalizing economy all represent nontraditional planning issues that corporations now must factor into the calculus of management decision making.

Internal Challenges

The responses to questions about companies' internal challenges are, perhaps, a sign of the times. Ten years ago, a similar survey would probably have elicited fewer references to cultural problems blocking the path to strategic success. But now, with the current focus on empowerment, John Kotter's linking corporate culture to performance, and Peter Senge's writings on the learning corporation, the emphasis on the role that culture plays in determining the effectiveness of strategy and strategic planning is not surprising. It is, however, highly significant and possibly the most important finding to emerge from this survey.

The Culture Challenge

With 38 mentions, culture clearly heads the array of corporate concerns in the field of strategic management. Virtually every respondent cited some aspect of this challenge, although the interpretation varied considerably from company to company. (Indeed, if one were to include in this category a number of mentions about management culture, which are currently counted under "Management Skills and Commitment," the coverage would be nearly 100 percent.) In broad terms, the references fell into one of three categories: problems, general attributes, and specific attributes.

Problems. In some cases, the focus was on undesirable traits that the company needs to remove in order that strategic management operate more effectively. For instance, respondents cited as barriers to change such personal traits as risk aversion, executives' turf concerns, and internal politics, and organizational problems such as bureaucracy, poor communications, and size. These problems are obstacles both to the development and, most particularly, to the implementation of strategy. One interesting observation—which many planners and executives will share—was that an organization is able to change radically only when it confronts a genuine crisis. In the absence of a real emergency, instilling a sense of impending crisis (even an imagined one) might be necessary to shake up corporate inertia.

General Attributes. Underlying respondents' references to the general traits or attributes that strategic management should seek to instill in a corporation were a willingness and ability to respond to change. At the most basic level, the corporate challenge is simply to generate a willingness to respond, quickly and effectively, to change. At the same time, as one respondent pointed out, enough stability must exist within the organization to provide a firm base from which to seal with change. Most individuals become ineffective in a state of total flux, so balancing stability and change becomes a key challenge for the executive intent on any program of organizational transformation. Several companies mentioned learning and empowerment as important corporate attributes. Given the pace and complexity of change in their business environments, more and more corporations are recognizing the following:

- Planning is more a matter of continuous organizational learning (scanning, interpreting, and adapting to environmental change) than it is of control.
- Corporate response to change can only be sufficiently rapid, flexible, and pervasive if responsibility filters down into and throughout the organization, maximizing employees' involvement and empowering them to take action.

A Japanese corporation used an anthropological analogy in describing the culture shift it saw was necessary. The Japanese culture, they noted, is fundamentally agricultural. What the Japanese need now—and what they are aiming for is a "mind change to a hunting culture." Whatever the merits of this interpretation of the Japanese culture, the analogy is interesting and provocative, particularly if one focuses on the attributes of a hunting band: relatively small size, independence, mobility, and team orientation.

Specific attributes. Not surprisingly, companies cited speed, flexibility, and enthusiasm as more specific attributes that they need to cultivate if strategy is to move from paper to the marketplace. Streamlining the organizational culture can achieve only so much toward these qualities. A change of attitudes—and behavior—must also take place if these attributes are to be embedded in corporate performance. Thus, culture change itself becomes as primary goal of strategic management. For example, revitalizing the corporate culture has been an essential part of Jack Welch's vision for GE. In stage one, which he accomplished relatively quickly (in three to four years), he flattened the structure and slimmed the organization. Stage two—the Work-Out program to achieve radical culture change—will necessarily be, As Welch himself had noted, a continuing crusade. That companies still recognize this need for change is, in itself, an indicator and an admission of the real magnitude of the effort required to break away from the ingrained internal bias that has characterized corporate bureaucracy for so long.

Management Skills and Commitment

For nearly half the respondents, the quality and role of top management emerged as significant challenges. The management problem—which firms see as antithetical to the broad strategic view necessary for success in today's competitive battles—evidently stems from the narrow focus and operational background of top managers. In a surprisingly frank appraisal of the limitation of today's senior management, respondents made frequent references to a lack of vision and leadership, an unclear (or uncommunicated) sense of strategic direction, and reactive (rather than the desired proactive) responses to change. In a few cases, respondents were concerned about senior managers' role in the strategic management process: their willingness to participate fully in strategy development and their ownership of, and commitment to, the strategies that evolve from this process. These two problems are, of course, connected: Without full participation in the development of strategy, no executive is going to have more than a lukewarm commitment to its execution. Fortunately, evidence suggests that these problems are diminishing in their incidence and intensity as responsibility for strategic management shifts from staff to line managers.

Financial Challenges

In this age of intensifying competition, traditional financial concerns rank high on the corporate agenda. More than one-third of the companies in the survey, citing these concerns among the most critical challenges they face, recognized the need to

- Reduce and control costs (both direct and overhead)
- Improve productivity and profitability
- Sharpen investment focus
- Improve portfolio management

These responses are not surprising. However, the careful attention that both company executives and the financial community pay to the placement of new chief financial officers—at IBM, Kodak and Chrysler, for instance, illustrates the importance of financial acumen and controls to a company's strategy.

Operational Problems

The appearance of operational problems on a list of strategic concerns serves as a solid reminder that strategic management is, or should be, concerned with both strategy and tactics. Indeed, five respondents expressed concern about the lack of coordination between operations and strategy, indicating that these two systems still operate separately rather than as meshed cogs in an integrated system. Other linkage problems that were mentioned by respondents were those between production and marketing and between R&D and operations. All together, such problems revealed a growing dissatisfaction with the traditional organization structure based on functions (and the problems of interfunctional coordination) and a slow movement toward organizing instead around processes (i.e., business process redesign—see Table A.3).

The Innovation Challenge

Along with speed and flexibility, innovation is perhaps the most desired quality in competitive performance today. Most respondents mentioned technological innovation (although a widespread need exists for creativity in all aspects of corporate performance) and recognized that, given the pace and global reach of technological development, a need exists to

- Improve the monitoring of R&D on a worldwide basis
- Increase external technology acquisition, recognizing that not even the largest corporation can be world class in every aspect of needed technology
- Speed new product development
- Improve management of the R&D portfolio

The growing importance of technology strategy (see Figure A.1) as an integral part of overall business strategy reflects the new importance of technological innovation in meeting these needs.

Strategic Planning Process

Companies no longer have the same obsession with process and methodology that they did 20 (or even 10) years ago, but there is still some lingering concern about some aspects of the process. Particular challenges include maintaining the credibility of the planning staff; the time commitment needed for a quality job; clarifying the respective roles of corporate and SBU strategy; improving the scanning and monitoring systems, especially in the domain of competitive intelligence; and, as always, tightening the link between strategic and operational planning.

THE BENEFITS OF STRATEGIC MANAGEMENT

Clearly, the ultimate measures of successful management are stakeholder satisfaction and corporate profitability, vitality, and competitive positioning. However, short of these benchmarks, a sound approach to strategic management can achieve gains in organizational clarity, drive, and efficiency. The responses to this survey make clear that companies have high hopes for strategic management. However, they also recognize that they still have far to go before realizing these benefits to the fullest.

Figure A.1
Dimensions of Change

What have been the major changes, in the past five to seven years, in your
company's approach to strategic planning and strategic management?

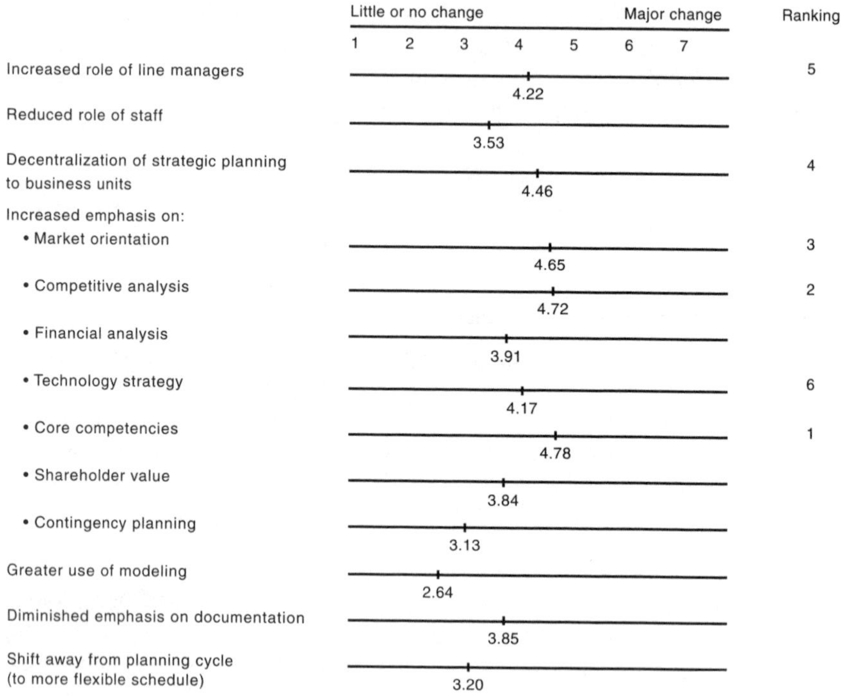

	Little or no change					Major change		Ranking
	1	2	3	4	5	6	7	
Increased role of line managers				4.22				5
Reduced role of staff			3.53					
Decentralization of strategic planning to business units				4.46				4
Increased emphasis on:								
• Market orientation				4.65				3
• Competitive analysis				4.72				2
• Financial analysis			3.91					
• Technology strategy				4.17				6
• Core competencies				4.78				1
• Shareholder value			3.84					
• Contingency planning			3.13					
Greater use of modeling		2.64						
Diminished emphasis on documentation			3.85					
Shift away from planning cycle (to more flexible schedule)			3.20					

Respondents identified three most highly rated benefits of strategic management (see Figure A.2):

- A clearer sense of strategic vision for the organization
- Sharper focus on what is strategically important, both in planning and
  implementation
- Improved understanding of a rapidly changing business environment

Close behind these benefits comes the still illusive goal of improved integration
of strategy and operations.

Respondents also offered their views as to how strategic management could
help in meeting the critical internal and external challenges they had identified
earlier in the survey.

Figure A.2
The Benefits of Strategic Management

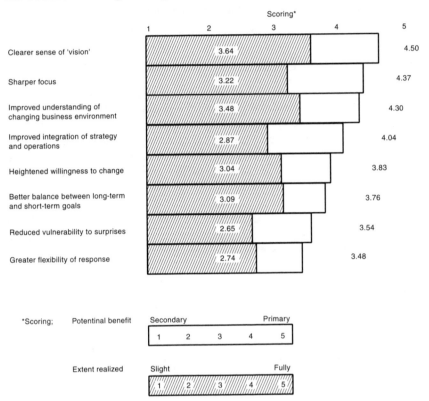

Responding to External Challenges

Strategic management provides a better understanding of the dynamics of change in the business environment to deal with external challenges and, one hopes, to reduce vulnerability to surprises. However, reduced vulnerability remains only a hope, and, whether from resignation or lack if effort, reduced vulnerability remains a low priority. Improved understanding of the business's externalities, on the other hand, is one of the three critical benefits that companies have more fully realized.

Responding to Internal Challenges

The list of the potential benefits of strategic management that deal with internal challenges is long. In addition to citing a clearer vision and a sharper focus, respondents referred to several cultural benefits—a heightened willingness to change, greater flexibility of response, better balance between long-term and short-term goals, and closer linkage between strategy and operations. Interestingly, three of these benefits—clearer vision, sharper focus, and improved integration—exhibit the largest gaps between actuality and potential, possibly once again underscoring the inherent difficulties in promoting cultural and organizational change.

THE ROLE OF CORPORATE PLANNING UNITS

Despite the decentralization of strategic planning to business units, there remains a valid role for corporate planning components. Overwhelmingly (with only four exceptions), companies said that they maintained a strategic planning capability at the corporate level. And the organizational positioning of this component is indicative of its perceived importance. In half the cases, the planning unit reports to the CEO, and in some Japanese companies, to a senior management committee; in most remaining companies, the planning unit reports to a senior (or executive) vice president.

The functions of the corporate planning component (see Table A.2) reflect a division of responsibilities between the corporate center and the decentralized SBUs. Appropriately, the key central responsibilities are the following:

Table A.2
The Responsibilities of Corporate-Level Planning Components

which functions is this component responsible?	Number of Responses* For	
	Yes	No
Economic forecasting	21	20
Market/competitive analysis	24	17
Strategic issues analysis	40	1
Strategy guidelines for SBUs	31	8
Corporate strategy development	33	6
Business development	16	25
Mergers/acquisitions analysis	20	17
SBU plans review	23	16
Corporate budgeting	6	33
Modeling	14	24

* Totals do not add to 46 because not all companies responded to each point

*Totals do not add to 46 because not all companies responded to each point.

- Identification and analysis of companywide strategic issues and the development of corporate responses to them
- Development of overall corporate strategies, such as portfolio investment priorities
- Drafting of planning guidelines (for example, economic and other assumptions, likely capital resource availability) for executive approval to assist SBUs in the development of their strategies and operating plans

However, if the lower rank of corporate budgeting is any indicator, planning appears to have outgrown its origins in the financial function, and its role as corporate inquisitor in reviewing SBU plans also seems to have diminished. Business development is more the responsibility of business units, whereas market and competitive analysis and mergers and acquisitions (M&A) analysis are shared functions of both corporate and SBU planning.

The size of corporate planning staffs has slimmed in recent years—a fact that this survey reflects. Setting aside two major Japanese companies, each of which reported a staff of 70, the average staff size is just under 10. Although reductions are in part the result of the general downsizing of corporate staff, strategic planning components in particular have shed responsibilities (and, some would say, power) both upward to senior management and downward to business units.

THE USE OF NEW METHODOLOGIES

Ten or more years ago, one of the major criticisms of strategic planning was its obsession with methodologies and its tendency to build the whole planning process around a single methodology. Despite a continuing tendency toward the latest fad in methodology, process, or approach, most corporate strategic planning now avoids the trap of overdependence on a single silver bullet. Indeed, the results shown in Table A.3 suggest that, on average, most companies employ four methodologies in their process—a finding that we should not interpret too literally, although it does provide encouraging evidence of a more sophisticated and comprehensive approach to what is perhaps the most difficult task confronting management.

The most frequently mentioned methodologies were scenario planning and core competencies analysis, with benchmarking close behind. The use of scenarios has been growing slowly since its introduction into the Royal Dutch/Shell system during the 1970s. More recently, it has received added impetus from the prevalence of shocks in the business environment and companies' growing admission of the need to come to grips with uncertainty in their planning. Core competencies and benchmarking are more recent arrivals on the planning scene and are the products of the new urgency to develop best practices and an organization's innate capabilities to their fullest in an effort to ensure competitive survival.

So far, the spread of time-based competition and business practice redesign

Table A.3
Principal Methodologies in Use in Strategic Planning

Methodology /Approach	General Use	Little or No Use
Total quality management	16	20
Shareholder value analysis	16	20
Time-based competition	9	**27**
Core competencies analysis	**26**	10
Scenario planning	**25**	11
Business process redesign	12	**24**
Benchmarking	**20**	16
Value chain analysis	16	20

Note: Only 36 of the 46 companies completed this
        section of the survey. Figures in bold highlight
        the greatest number of responses.

Note: Only 36 of the 46 companies completed this section of the survey. Figures in bold highlight the greatest number of responses.

has been decidedly limited. This fact may, however, be due to the relative novelty of these approaches. Certainly, a reading of the management literature would suggest that they are both destined to much greater use in the future.

CONCLUDING OBSERVATIONS

Despite the survey's limitations—the size of the sample, the restrictive nature of the questionnaire, and the fact that researchers have many follow-up questions yet to ask—its results do lead to a number of overall conclusions about the current state of strategic planning/management in the Triad countries (North America, Japan, and Europe).

First, and most important, strategic planning is clearly being transformed into strategic management; that is, it is moving

- Away from being largely staff driven, heavily dependent on analytical methodologies and elaborate documentation, and focused on the development of plans

- Toward becoming executive driven, balancing hard (quantitative) and soft (judgmental) tools and approaches, and focusing on action and the implementation of strategies

The whole strategic planning process has been driven down into the organization, with much of the activity taking place in business units rather than at the corporate level (although corporate planning components are still the norm, albeit with truncated responsibilities.

The evidence suggests that this transition is far from complete. Most companies report that they are far from realizing the full potential of their strategic planning systems. However, the transition has progressed sufficiently far to have gained executive acceptance of the importance of strategic management. This acceptance stems in part from the increasing need to think strategically about the external and internal challenges confronting corporations, and in part from the increased involvement, and hence ownership, of line managers in the process.

In comparison to its record at the end of the 1980s, strategic management is now a far more effective instrument for shaping the course of a corporation or business unit. This increase in effectiveness starts with much more sophisticated and holistic thinking about the truly strategic issues, gains power from a more thorough and patient examination of options, and gathers further momentum from more careful linking of strategy to operational implementation. All told, the emphasis is now on results rather than format and on making a difference in corporate performance rather than making an impression on the board of directors.

One indicator of this increased sophistication is the greater selectivity in the choice of planning methodologies. Not only do companies rely far less than they did 10 to 15 years ago on a single methodology—such as the growth-share matrix or the experience curve—they now employ a mix of methodologies as the needs and planning culture of the corporation determine. A pronounced shift is also occurring to methodologies, such as scenario planning and total quality management, that are less mechanistic in their approach and more sensitive to the critical uncertainty of many of the variable that planning must address.

Perhaps the most provocative finding, however, is the growing emphasis on organization and culture as critical ingredients in the execution of strategy. This emphasis has not come about at the expense of external analysis; indeed, the survey indicates a broad awareness of the external challenges of today's business environment. Rather, the attention to culture represents perhaps the greatest departure from the past and is all the more surprising for being an essentially soft factor in a process prone to rely on hard analyses. Culture is, in effect, the internal equivalent of the customer orientation in the corporation's outward-facing posture. It represents a recognition that the values, motivation, and behavior of the organization's members are critical determinants of corporate performance—and of the success or failure in implementing strategy.

Appendix B

SCHOOLS OF STRATEGIC THINKING

In their book, *Strategy Safari: A Guided Tour through the Wilds of Strategic Management*, Mintzberg, Ahlstrand, and Lampel identify 10 views of the strategy process that have been popularized by academics, consultants, or business executives, each taking a highly focused view, all too often disconnected from each other.

The Design School

This view sees strategy formation as a process to achieve the optimum fit between a company's strengths and weaknesses and the external opportunities and threats that it faces. Senior executives formulate the strategy in a deliberate process of conscious thought (neither formally analytical nor informally intuitive) so that operating managers can implement it.

The Planning School

This school reflects most of the design school's assumptions except a rather significant one: that the process is not just cerebral, but formal, decomposable into distinct steps, delineated by checklists, supported by techniques, and controlled by staff planners.

The Positioning School

In this view, popularized by Michael Porter in the 1980s, strategy can be reduced to generic positions (e.g., product differentiation, low cost) through formalized analyses of industry situations. Hence planners become analysts.

The Entrepreneurial School

The entrepreneurial school focuses the process on the chief executive officer, as the design school does, but, unlike that school, it roots strategy largely in intuition. That shifts strategies from precise designs and plans to more amorphous visions, or perspectives, typically couched in terms of metaphors.

The Cognitive School

Academic research has increased steadily on the role of cognitive biases in strategy making and on cognition as information processing. A newer branch of this school adopted a more subjective view of the strategy process: that cognition is used to construct strategies as creative interpretations rather than simply to map reality in some more or less objective way.

The Learning School

Dating back to incrementalism (the notion of a series of nibbles rather than one big bite), as well as concepts such as emergent strategy (growing out of individual decisions rather than immaculately conceived), a model of strategy making as learning developed that differed from earlier schools. In this view, strategies are emergent, strategists can be found throughout the organization, and so-called formulation and implementation intertwine.

The Power School

This school focuses on strategy making rooted in power, in two senses. Micropower sees the development of strategies within the organization as essentially political, a process involving bargaining, persuasion, and confrontation among inside actors. Macropower takes the organization as an entity that uses its power over others and among its partners in alliances, joint ventures, and other network relationships to negotiate collective strategies in its interests.

The Cultural School

The reverse image of power is culture. Whereas one focuses on self-interest and implementation, the other focuses on common interests and integration strategy formation as a social process rooted in culture. Culture became a big issue in U.S. management thinking after the impact of Japanese management was fully realized in the 1980s, and it became clear that strategic advantage can be the product of unique cultural factors that are difficult to imitate.

The Environmental School

Mintzberg, Ahlstrand, and Lampel single out the environmental school (although it is perhaps not strictly strategic management) for the light it throws on the demands of the environment. They include in this category so-called contingency theory, which considers what responses are expected of organizations that face particular environmental conditions, and population ecology, writings that place severe limits on strategic choice.

The Configuration School

One side of this school, more academic and descriptive, sees organization as configuration, coherent clusters of characteristics and behaviors, and so serves as one way to integrate the claims of the other schools: each configuration, in effect, in its own place—planning, for example, in machine-type organizations in conditions of relative stability, or entrepreneurship under more dynamic conditions of start-up and turnaround. If organizations can be described by such states, then change must be described as rather dramatic transformation—the leap from one state to another. And so a literature and practice of transformation, more prescriptive and practitioner oriented, developed as the other side of this coin.

Appendix C

GLOSSARY OF TERMS USED IN STRATEGIC PLANNING

Business environment: The complex interaction of dynamic forces and trends in the macroenvironment (social, economic, political/regulatory, and technological factors) and the microenvironment (specific market, industry, and competitive factors) that directly influence a business's goals, strategies, policies, and actions.

Business unit: A coherent component of a company responsible for managing all aspects of a clearly defined line of products and/or services in a given market and with profit-and-loss responsibility for integrating both long-term strategy and short-term operations. Also called *strategic business unit* or *line of business.*

Goals: Specific, usually quantifiable and measurable steps toward achieving the business's strategic objectives.

Issue: A current or prospective opportunity or threat arising out of internal or external trends or developments that would have a major impact on the business (its strategies, policies, growth, or profitability) and on which corporate action can have some influence. Also called *strategic issue.*

Mission: A statement that identifies the basic purpose of the business, defines the arena in which it will operate and the customers it will serve, and sets broad objectives.

Objectives: Broad aims, both financial and nonfinancial, defining what the business seeks to achieve (or avoid) in implementing its mission (companies sometimes distinguish between long-term and short-term objectives).

Options: A range of structurally different (and mutually exclusive) strategies, among which executives must choose, to address key strategic issues and achieve desired goals and objectives. Also called *strategy options* or *strategy alternatives*.

Scenarios: Frameworks for structuring management's perceptions about alternative future environments in which executive decisions might be played out, or, simply, stories of different plausible futures that might evolve from uncertainties in key forces in the business environment.

Stakeholders: The individuals and groups with an interest (stake) in the policies and practices of a business/company, including share owners, customers, employees, suppliers, dealers, and distributors, as well as communities in which the company operates, the public at large and its representatives (in the legislative and administrative branches of government), and in some cases, competitors (through joint ventures and alliances).

Strategic management: Management of a business according to a coherent vision and a driving strategy to achieve it; a system that emphasizes running the business as a continuous iteration of planning, decision making, resource allocation, and execution that integrates functional strategies, internalities, and externalities, and long-term and short-term goals using strategy and vision as a guide.

Strategy: The driving force that shapes the future nature and direction of the business; it defines the means that will be employed to achieve the corporate vision.

SW/OTs: An acronym for strengths and weaknesses (of the business) and the opportunities and threats (presented by the business environment) that become apparent in strategic planning analyses.

Values statement: An articulation of the corporate values that serves as the guiding principle for corporate actions and ethical behavior, defines the character of its relations with stakeholders, and establishes management style and corporate culture.

Vision: A coherent and dynamic statement of what a company (or business) can—and should—become in the future (the time horizon varying with the nature of the business); a fairly detailed picture of the business's future scope, scale, market and competitive focus, image and stakeholder relationships, and organizational structure and culture.

Appendix D

STATOIL: A CASE STUDY IN SCENARIO PLANNING

The best way to understand how scenario planning works is to follow it, step by step, through an actual case study. I have chosen the case of Statoil, the Norwegian state-owned oil and gas company, with whom I worked as a consultant while I was with SRI International. Statoil—den norske stats oljeselskap a.s., to give the company its full and formal title—makes a good case to learn from because the project was well focused and the process was straightforward. In addition, the lapse of time (more than 10 years) since this project started gives the reader the privilege of judging how well (or not!) the scenarios covered the uncertainties of the time as they worked out in reality.

We started the project in 1987, which was a year of volatile oil prices. The near-collapse of international financial markets occurred on Black Monday (October 19, 1987). It was a year in which it was all too easy to be, as one team member put it at the time, "whipsawed by events."

The management mindset at Statoil, as in most integrated oil and gas companies, was in a state of seeming contradiction. Their thinking was a curious mix of certainty and uncertainty—uncertainty about the timing and strength of oil shocks, but near certainty about the underlying strength of a seller's market and about the continuing preeminence of oil in Norway's economy. Scenarios were seen as a way to cushion the severity of oil shocks by instilling what-if thinking and contingency planning into the group's strategic management.

This was the setting, then, for a trial run to explore the use of scenarios in developing a long-term research and development strategy for Statoil's Exploration and Production (E&P) Division. Scenarios were far from being the whole of this project; but they were the key to helping R&D managers deal with the inevitable uncertainties they faced in thinking through such a strategy. Much of this uncertainty stems from high-impact social, political, economic, and technological forces and the consequences they have for the business and, thus, on its technological needs. Oil and gas prices are an obvious example, and for Statoil, so are the strength of the Norwegian economy and the availability of technical skills. But the questions do not end there:

- How important will the oil industry be in the nation's future?
- What role will technology play in such a future?
- What kind of technologies will the Division have to master in the E&P environment of the future?

Step 1: Defining the Decision Focus for the Project (i.e., What Is the Decision to Be Made at the Conclusion of the Scenarios?)

In delineating the scope of the project, we determined that there were four defining issues to consider. The project should do the following:

- Deal explicitly and effectively with the full range of uncertainty in the long-term future.
- Take account of future corporate, competitive, and technological conditions.
- Be compatible with existing planning and management culture.
- Be capable of developing a range of plausible technology strategy options.

With these issues in mind, we framed the decision-focus question as follows:

"Which technologies should the E&P Division pursue most strongly in order to best serve long-term business needs?"

We determined that the scenarios would have to focus on the future industry and technological environment of the E&P Division, including the structure both of the oil and gas market and of Statoil's competition. Given the global nature of the oil and gas industry, the scenarios would be global in nature but take into account key aspects of Norway's social, political, and economic situation. Technology was also singled out for specific analysis in view of the project's focus on R&D strategy. We set the time-horizon for the scenarios as the next 20 years (1990–2010) to accommodate the long lead time and long-term payoff of technology. Ultimately, of course, the R&D strategy would have to address both the short-term and long-term needs of the Division.

In a parallel analysis performed at the same time, we conducted an assessment of the Division's current technology portfolio in terms of its linkage to the attainment of current Statoil/Division goals. This assessment had no bearing on the scenario development work itself but played a major role later on (step 6) when we examined the strategic implications of the scenarios.

Step 2: Identifying the Key Decision Factors (i.e., What Are the Key Elements of the Future That We Would Like to Know in order to Improve the Quality of Our Decision?)

In order to determine the optimum long-term technology portfolio for the Division, we reasoned that we would benefit from having answers to five simple questions:

- What will be the Division's operating and R&D needs?
- What will Statoil's competitors do? How successful will they be?
- What will be the sources and availability of technology, R&D funding, and human resources? How should the Division tap them?
- How will Statoil's charter and government regulations and policies influence the Division's R&D strategy?
- What will be the scope of the research network? How should the Division utilize it?

This listing then led us to identify seven key decision factors that the scenarios would have to focus on and shed some light on their possible future trajectories:

- E&P operator needs, including future levels of exploration and production; the geographic distribution, and geologic characteristics, of E&P activities; and the mix between oil and gas
- Competition from other oil companies, including their major strategic thrusts; the extent of their emphasis on strategic alliances and joint ventures; and their R&D strategies and successes (e.g., number of breakthroughs)
- Availability of R&D funding—internally, and from the Norwegian government and R&D partners
- Availability of technology—in other companies, universities, and research organizations
- Availability of needed professional skills (in the Norwegian labor market)
- Statoil's relations with the Norwegian government, including Statoil's charter with respect to its economic development role, its resource production role, and safety and environmental regulations
- Relations with research organizations, both in Norway and internationally

Step 3: Identifying and Assessing the Key External Forces

Given the scope and complexity of the global, national, industry, and market environment involved in this project, it is not surprising that the scenario team identified more than 60 forces that had some bearing, directly or indirectly, on these seven key decision factors. In total, these forces represent a conceptual model of the dynamics of the Division's industry and technology environment.

Clearly some sorting out of such an array of forces was called for, partly because of the unwieldiness of trying to manipulate this many elements in our model, but mainly because not all the forces were equally important or equally uncertain. We therefore put them through an impact/uncertainty screen in order to single out the high-impact/high-uncertainty factors and, as a result, we were left with 35 forces in this category.

While this assessment might seem to represent an unusually high degree of uncertainty about the future, it was perhaps not surprising, given the nature of the global oil and gas business.

Step 4: Establishing the Scenario Logics

Scenario logics are the critical axes of uncertainty and the organizing principles around which the scenarios are developed. Our search for a simplified logical structure for the scenarios led us into a prolonged discussion of these 35 forces. We looked for groupings, cause-and-effect relationships, and other linkages among these forces. In the end, we concluded that, for the R&D decision confronting the Division, the truly critical uncertainties clustered around three axes of uncertainty:

- *The structure of the energy market (supply and demand).* Will there be a return to a seller's market, or will the (then current) buyer's market continue?
- *The Norwegian economy.* Will the economy continue to be heavily energy dependent, or will it successfully restructure into a more diversified form?
- *Technology.* Will technology evolve, in the general economy and in energy industries, in a fragmented and somewhat incremental manner, or will a more integrated and accelerated evolution take place?

The alternate outcomes for each axis were, we felt, supported by logic and did present radically different, but rational, views of the way the world might work. This structure for the scenarios did, therefore, push the envelop of uncertainty to its plausible limits.

Step 5: Selecting and Elaborating the Scenarios

From among the eight scenarios that these three axes of uncertainty made possible, we selected four for study because we felt this was the most the decision-making system could assimilate. These four scenarios effectively covered the critical area of planning uncertainty and met the necessary criteria, namely, the following:

1. The selected scenarios should be plausible: that is, they must fall within the limits of what might reasonably be expected to happen.
2. They should be structurally different: that is, they are not so close to one another that they become simply variations of a base case.
3. They must be *internally consistent:* that is, the combination of logics in a scenario must not have any built-in inconsistency that would undermine the credibility of the scenario.
4. They should have decision-making utility; that is, each scenario, and all the scenarios as a set, should contribute useful insights into the future that will bear on the decision focus that has been selected.
5. The scenarios should challenge the organization's conventional wisdom in the way it looks at the future.

Scenario A: The Nation's Future Is Dominated by the Oil and Gas Economy The key drivers of this scenario are a seller's market in energy, an energy-dependent Norwegian economy, and fragmented/incremental technology development. Traditional patterns of industrial and technological development result in a continuing high level of energy dependence. As a consequence, oil prices rebound and the Organization of Petroleum Exporting Countries (OPEC) regains dominance about 1995. The nation debates restructuring its economy, but the actions proposed and taken are not sufficient to divert the strong push toward further development of national oil and gas resources.

Scenario B: Oil and Gas Benefits Lead to a Restructured National Economy The key drivers of this scenario are a seller's market in energy, diversified restructuring of the Norwegian economy, and integrated/accelerated technology development. A more rapid diffusion of new technology (materials, computers, communications) and the gradual reduction of budget and trade deficits result in higher levels of growth worldwide and closer political and economic relationships among nations. The Organization for Economic Cooperation and Development (OECD) countries continue to maintain a high level of energy dependence, thus ensuring the return of a seller's market. Norway uses technology and national oil and gas revenues for energy resource development and the diversification of the economy.

Scenario C: The Country Struggles in a Depressed World The key drivers of this scenario are a buyer's market in energy, an energy-dependent Norwegian economy, and fragmented/incremental technology development. Structural problems in both developed and developing countries reach a crisis and, lacking resolution, result in a prolonged worldwide recession. Commodity and energy prices plunge, and the politics of protectionism and national self-sufficiency help to generate a siege mentality in many countries. Under these pressures, Norway seeks to leverage her energy resource advantage into a strategy for national economic survival.

Scenario D: The Country Is Driven from Oil Dependence by Global Restructuring The key drivers of this scenario are a buyer's market in energy, diversified restructuring of the Norwegian economy, and integrated/accelerated technology development. This scenario represents the furthest evolution of a globalized economy and the information society. High-tech breakthroughs in such areas as information technology, biotechnology, and materials radically change the structure, mix, and location of global economic activity. The dependence of the economy on raw material and energy declines dramatically, and information-based value increases correspondingly. In this high-growth but highly competitive world, Norway has no choice but to restructure its economy.

A tabular comparison of the scenarios, covering approximately half of the more than 60 forces included in the conceptual model of the Division's environment, provided a detailed look inside each of the scenarios, enabling decision makers to make point-by-point comparison of the differing conditions that the E&P Division might encounter.

Step 6: Interpreting the Scenarios

One problem with scenario planning has been that managers generally find it easier to imagine how the world might change than to confront the need to change their organizations. In this project, we recognized this problem and sought to deal with it by the way we structured this sixth step.

To start the process of preparing for the future, the project team met for an intensive weeklong workshop. During the first four days, the team discussed the implications of the scenarios, selecting a different scenario each day for consideration. Addressing a different scenario each day, the team was able to immerse itself in the details of one scenario at a time and thus complete its evaluation before moving on to the next scenario and a different outlook on the future.

Then, on day five, we reviewed the results of the first four days of discussion to identify the commonalities and differences of the four scenarios. To focus our thinking, we needed to refer to the key decision factors that had formed the original decision focus for the scenarios. These gave rise to a series of questions that formed a natural linkage between the scenarios and the development of R&D strategy:

- What will be the Division's R&D needs?

- What will Statoil's competitors be doing? How successful are they likely to be?

- What will be the sources and availability of technology, R&D funding, and human resources? And how should Statoil tap them?

- How will Statoil's charter, and the government's regulations and policies, influence the R&D strategy?
- What is the scope of Statoil's research network? And how should they utilize it?

At this stage, the exercise proceeded in five discrete steps:

1. Review each scenario description. This was the process of increasing our intellectual and, just as importantly, our emotional involvement in the conditions of a given scenario. This step was not simply a review of the material we had earlier developed. It required an attempt to step into the scenario so that we could believe that it was the future and that we were part of it.

2. Assess implications of the scenario. With the description of the scenario clearly in mind, the team then discussed the effect of the scenario on the key decision factors. To help the discussion, we developed a more extensive list of questions to answer. For example, under "E&P Operator Needs," we asked "Which geographic areas of exploration will be most emphasized? Will certain geologic field types have more or less emphasis?"

3. Identify the best strategy, opportunities, and threats. The focus here was on answering three questions:

   - What seems the best strategy for dealing with this scenario?
   - What are the major opportunities and threats inherent in the scenario?
   - What should Statoil do—and not do?

   To stress the what-if nature of our thinking at this point, we used as a lead-in the following phrase: "If we could forecast the future with certainty and know that this scenario would develop as it has been described, then Statoil should . . . . " (name a specific action).

4. Evaluate the scenario's impact on the Division's goals. Earlier, we had assessed the linkage between R&D programs and the Division's goals (see step 1). That is, we determined which programs contributed how much to the accomplishment of which goals. Here we wanted to assess what changes might be made in company and Division goals in light of the external conditions represented by the scenario. Important questions were as follows: Which goals might be emphasized, and which might be dropped or changed? What new goals might be adopted?

5. Develop a portfolio of priority R&D programs. Now, having a sense of what the major opportunities and threats might be, and how the company might change its business goals, we could use the linkages between R&D programs and business goals to reorder the R&D pri-

orities and so develop a research portfolio best attuned to the demands of that scenario.

Finally, we identified a set of four technology strategy options that were submitted to management for their evaluation and decision:

Strategy Option	Objective	Action
1. Low-cost strategy	Be competitive through cost leadership	Use technology to create low-cost solutions, and sacrifice some technical flexibility
2. Growth strategy	Strengthen position in seller's market	Expand programs that help maximize production, and de-emphasize future flexibility
3. Struggle strategy	Survival in hard times	Concentrate on programs with high payoff in downturns, and de-emphasize future flexibility
4. Resilient strategy	Be competitive in wide range of conditions	Develop broad technology base, and emphasize technical flexibility

Appendix E

STRATEGIC PLANNING
METHODOLOGIES

In recent years, the Boston-based consulting firm Bain & Company has published an annual survey of senior managers and management literature to identify 25 of the most popular and pertinent management tools. The company defines the tools and conducts detailed surveys to examine managers' use of tools and their success rates. The following list is taken from the 2000 survey, *Management Tools and Techniques: An Executive's Guide, 2000* (published by Bain & Company):

Activity-based management	One-to-one marketing
Balanced scorecard	Outsourcing
Benchmarking	Pay-for-performance
Core competencies	Real options analysis
Customer retention	reengineering
Customer satisfaction measurement	Scenario planning
Customer segmentation	Shareholder value analysis
Cycle time reduction	Strategic alliances
Growth strategies	Strategic planning
Knowledge management	Supply chain integration
Market disruption analysis	Total quality management
Merger integration teams	Virtual teams
Mission and vision statements	

Another listing of 30 methodologies was published in an article by James L. Webster, William E. Reif, and Jeffrey S. Bracker, "The Manager's Guide to Strategic Planning Tools and Techniques," in *Planning Review* (November/December, 1989) (Note: this journal is now called *Strategy & Leadership.*):

Dialectic inquiry	Future studies
Nominal group technique	Multiple scenarios
Delphi technique	Systematic procedure for identification of relevant environments (SPIRE)
Focus groups	Environmental scanning/forecasting
Driving force	Experience curves
Stakeholder analysis	Competitive analysis
Simulation technique	Portfolio analysis
PIMS analysis	Financial models analysis
Market opportunity analysis	Metagame analysis
Value chain analysis	Strategic gap analysis
Benchmarking	McKinsey 7-S analysis
Situational analysis (SW/OTs)	Operating budgets
Critical success factors/Strategic issues analysis	Management by objectives
Product life cycle analysis	Sustainable growth model
Product/market analysis	Strategic funds programming

BIBLIOGRAPHY

The literature on strategy and strategic planning is, as I have noted, vast and diverse, and the listing here is obviously only a tiny sampling of that outpouring. It does, however, represent the books—over a nearly 40-year period, from Ken Andrews and Igor Ansoff in the 1960s to Jack Welch and Adrian Slywotzky in the opening years of the new century—that have particularly influenced my own thinking on the subject. For readers who would like a more complete bibliography, I recommend that they consult the extensive list of references contained in Henry Mintzberg's two volumes listed here—*The Rise and Fall of Strategic Planning* and *Strategy Safari: A Guided Tour through the Wilds of Strategic Management.*

Andrews, Kenneth R. *The Concept of Corporate Strategy.* Homewood, Ill.: Irwin, 1965.

Ansoff, H. Igor. *Corporate Strategy.* New York: McGraw Hill, 1965.

———. *Implementing Strategic Management.* Englewood Cliffs, N.J.: Prentice-Hall, 1988.

Bossidy, Lawrence A. "Some Thoughts on Strategic Thinking." Speech presented to the Strategic Management Society, Boston, 14 October 1987.

Bossidy, Lawrence A., and Ram Charan. *Execution: The Discipline of Getting Things Done.* New York: Crown Business/Random House, 2002.

Brazen, John M., ed. *Strategic Management in Public and Voluntary Services: A Reader.* Kidlington, Oxford, U.K.: Elsevier Science Ltd., 1999.

Courtney, Hugh. *20/20 Foresight: Crafting Strategy in an Uncertain World.* Boston: Harvard Business School Press, 2001.

Cvitkovic, Emilio. "A Methodology to Analyze Competitors' Skills: Performance Profiles." *Competition: Forms, Facts and Fiction.* London: The Macmillan Press, Ltd., 1993.

Fahey, Liam, and Robert M. Randall, eds. *Portable MBA in Strategy.* 2d ed. New York: John Wiley & Sons, 2001.

Financial Times (London). *Mastering Strategy.* 12-part series of articles. 27 September 1999–13 December 1999.

Foster, Richard, and Sarah Kaplan. *Creative Destruction: Why Companies That Are Built to Last Underperform the Market—And How to Successfully Transform Them.* New York: Doubleday, 2001.

Freedman, Mike. "Building a Culture for Strategy." *Strategic Direction* 16, no. 2.

Gleick, James. *Chaos: Making of a New Science.* New York: Viking Penguin, Inc., 1987.

Grove, Andy. *Only the Paranoid Survive.* New York: Currency/Doubleday, 1996.

Guth, William D., ed. *Handbook of Business Strategy.* Boston: Warren, Gorham & Lamont, 1985.

Hamel, Gary. *Leading the Revolution.* Boston: Harvard Business School Press, 2000.

———. "Smart Mover, Dumb Mover." *Fortune,* 3 September 2001.

———. "What CEOs Can Learn from America." *Fortune,* 12 November 2001.

Hamel, Gary, and C. K. Prahalad. *Competing for the Future.* Boston: Harvard Business School Press, 1994.

Hammer, Michael, and James Champy. *Reengineering the Corporation: A Manifesto for Business Revolution.* New York: Harper Business, 1994.

Kotter, John P., and James L. Heskett. *Corporate Culture and Performance.* New York: Free Press, 1992.

London, Simon. "Diversity's Big Drawback." *Financial Times,* 25 January 2002.

Lovins, Amory B., L. Hunter Lovins, and Paul Hawken. "A Road Map for Natural Capitalism." *Harvard Business Review* (May–June 1999).

Manning, Tony. *Making Sense of Strategy.* New York: AMACOM, American Management Association, 2002.

Michael, Donald. *On Learning to Plan and Planning to Learn.* San Francisco: Jossey Bass, 1973.

Mintzberg, Henry. *The Rise and Fall of Strategic Planning.* New York: Free Press, 1994.

Mintzberg, Henry, Bruce Ahlstrand, and Joseph Lampel. *Strategy Safari: A Guided Tour through the Wilds of Strategic Management.* New York: Free Press, 1998.

"The New Breed of Strategic Planner," *Business Week.* 17 September 1984.

Pascale, Richard Tanner. *Managing on the Edge: How the Smartest Companies Use Conflict to Stay Ahead.* New York: Touchstone/Simon & Schuster, 1990.

Petersen, Marvin W., David D. Dill, Lisa A. Mets, and associates, eds. *Planning and Management for a Changing Environment.* San Francisco: Jossey-Bass Inc., 1997.

Porter, Michael E. "Caught in the Net," interview, *Business Week,* 27 August 2001.

———. *Competitive Strategy: Techniques for Analyzing Industries and Competitors.* New York: Free Press, 1980.

———. "Corporate Strategy: The State of Strategic Thinking." *The Economist* (23 May 1987): 17–22.

Porter, Michael E., and Claas van der Linde. "Green **and** Competitive." *Harvard Business Review,* September–October 1995.

Rigby, Darrell K. *Management Tools and Techniques: An Executive's Guide, 2000.* Boston: Bain & Company, 1999.

Schein, Edgar H. *The Corporate Culture Survival Guide.* San Francisco: Jossey-Bass Publishers, 1999.

Senge, Peter M. *The Fifth Discipline: The Art and Practice of the Learning Organization.* New York: Currency Doubleday, 1990.

Shepard, Stephen. Interview. *Business Week,* 28 January 2002.

Shrader, Ralph W., and Mike McConnell. "Security and Strategy in the Age of Discontinuity." *Strategy + Business* (first quarter 2002).

Slywotzky, Adrian, and David Morrison. "Becoming a Digital Business: It's Not about Technology." *Strategy and Leadership* (March/April 2001).

Steinbock, Dan. *The Nokia Revolution.* New York: American Management Association, 2001.

Stern, Carl W., and George Stalk, Jr., eds. *Perspectives on Strategy from the Boston Consulting Group.* New York: John Wiley & Sons, 1998.

Tregoe, Benjamin B., and John W. Zimmerman. *Top Management Strategy: What It Is and How to Make It Work.* New York: Simon and Schuster, 1980.

"The View from IBM: Lou Gerstner Does Have a Vision." *Business Week,* 30 October 1995.

Wack, Pierre. "Scenarios: Uncharted Waters Ahead." *Harvard Business Review,* September–October 1985.

Webster, James L., William E. Reif, and Jeffrey S. Bracker. "The Manager's Guide to Strategic Planning Tools and Techniques." *Planning Review* (November/December 1989): 4 ff.

Welch, Jack, with John A. Byrne. *Jack: Straight from the Gut.* New York: Warner Business Books, 2001.

Wilson, Ian. *The New Rules of Corporate Conduct: Rewriting the Social Charter.* Westport, Conn.: Quorum Books, 2000.

———. "Societal Change and the Planning Process." Presented at the AAAS Annual Meeting. New York, 31 January 1975.

"Yes, You Can Manage Long Term." *Fortune,* 21 November 1988.

Youngblood, Mark D. "Winning Cultures for the New Economy." *Strategy & Leadership,* November/December 2000, 4–9.

INDEX

About the Author

IAN WILSON is an international management consultant, author, and authority on scenario planning and strategic management. Principal of Wolf Enterprises, a consultancy in San Rafael, California, he started his career in England and later joined General Electric (GE) in the United States. At GE, as a member of the strategic planning staff, he established their pioneering Business Environmental Analysis component before becoming a public policy advisor to GE's chief executive officer. Later, as a senior management consultant with SRI International, he worked with senior management teams in a variety of industries.